NEW YORK TIMES BESTSELLING AUTHOR

KAILYN LOWRY'S

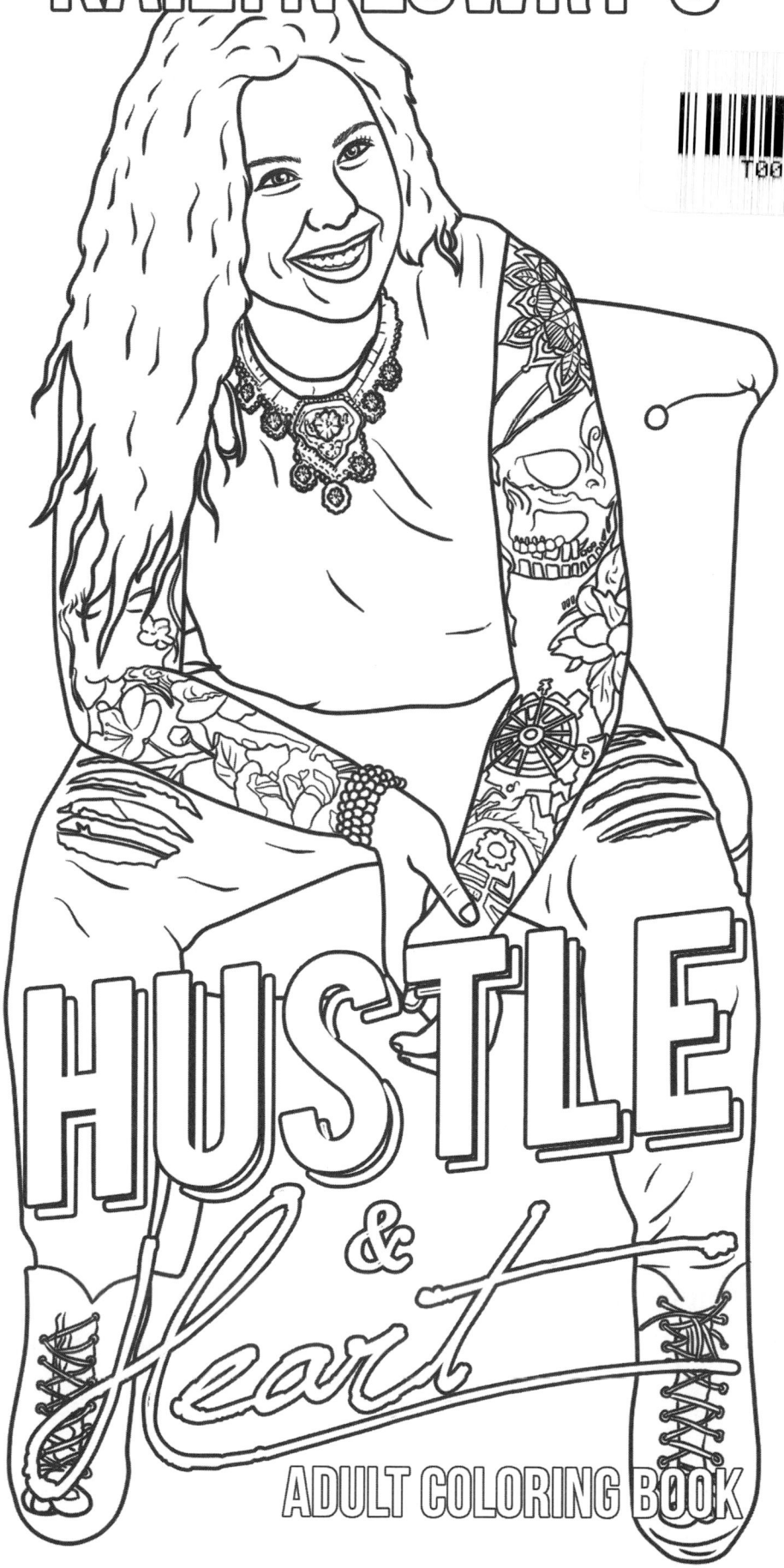

ADULT COLORING BOOK

T0060678

A POST HILL PRESS BOOK

Kailyn Lowry's Hustle and Heart Adult Coloring Book
© 2016 by Kailyn Lowry
All Rights Reserved

ISBN: 978-1-68261-164-7

No part of this book may be reproduced, stored in a retrieval system, or transmitted by any means without the written permission of the author and publisher.

Interior layout by Greg Johnson, Textbook Perfect

Post Hill
PRESS
Post Hill Press
posthillpress.com

Printed in the United States of America

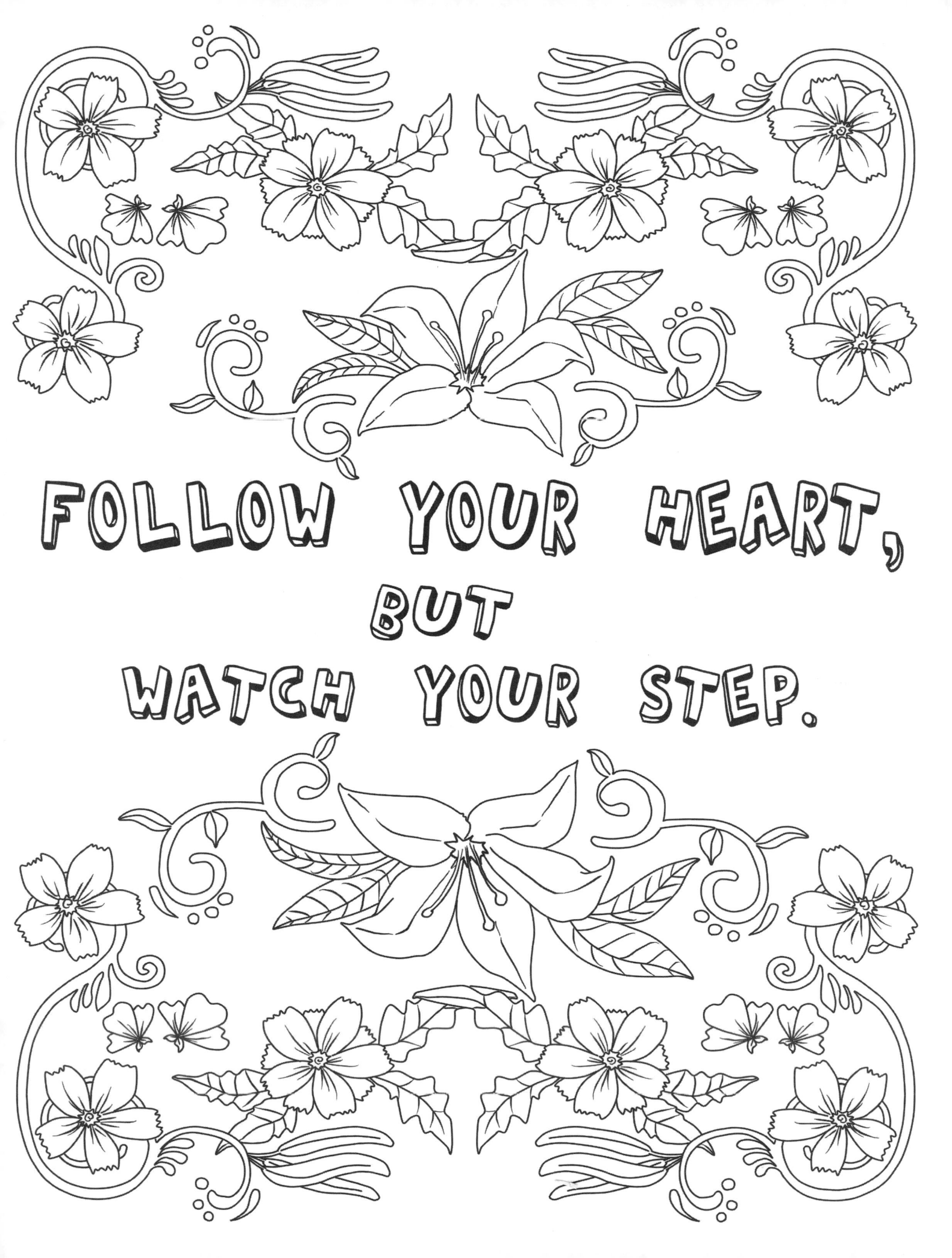
FOLLOW YOUR HEART,
BUT
WATCH YOUR STEP.

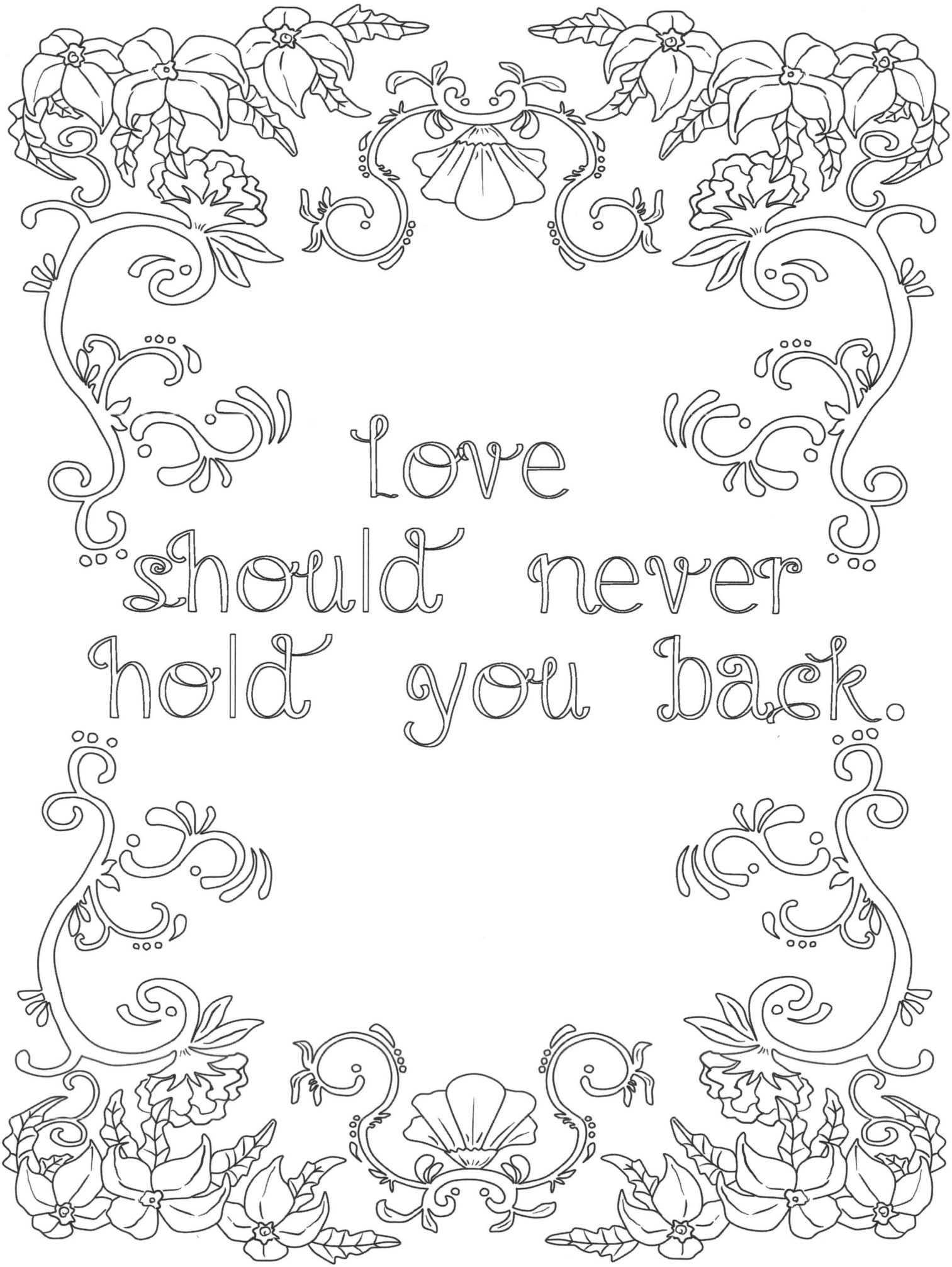
Love
should never
hold you back.

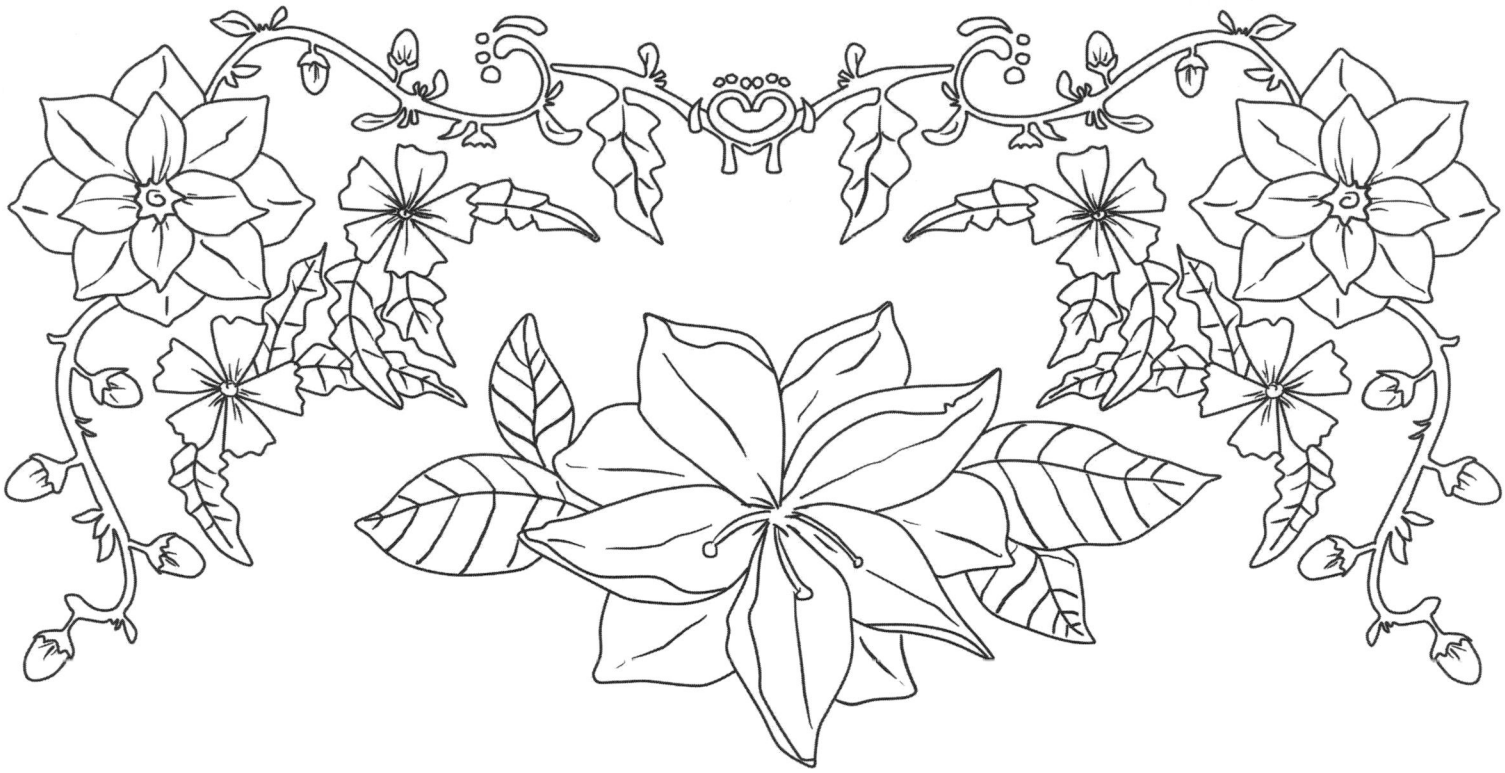

Loving yourself
is a superpower.

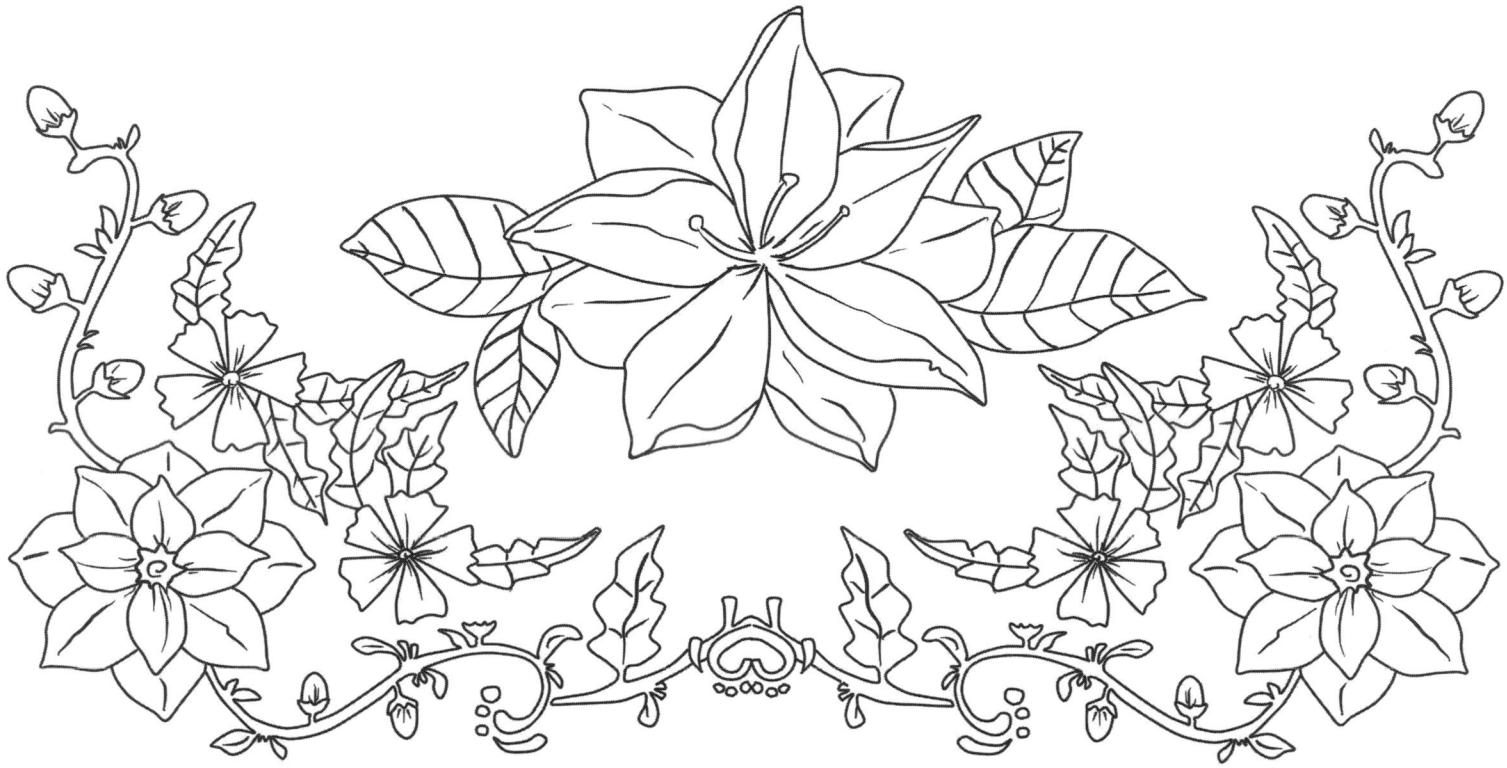

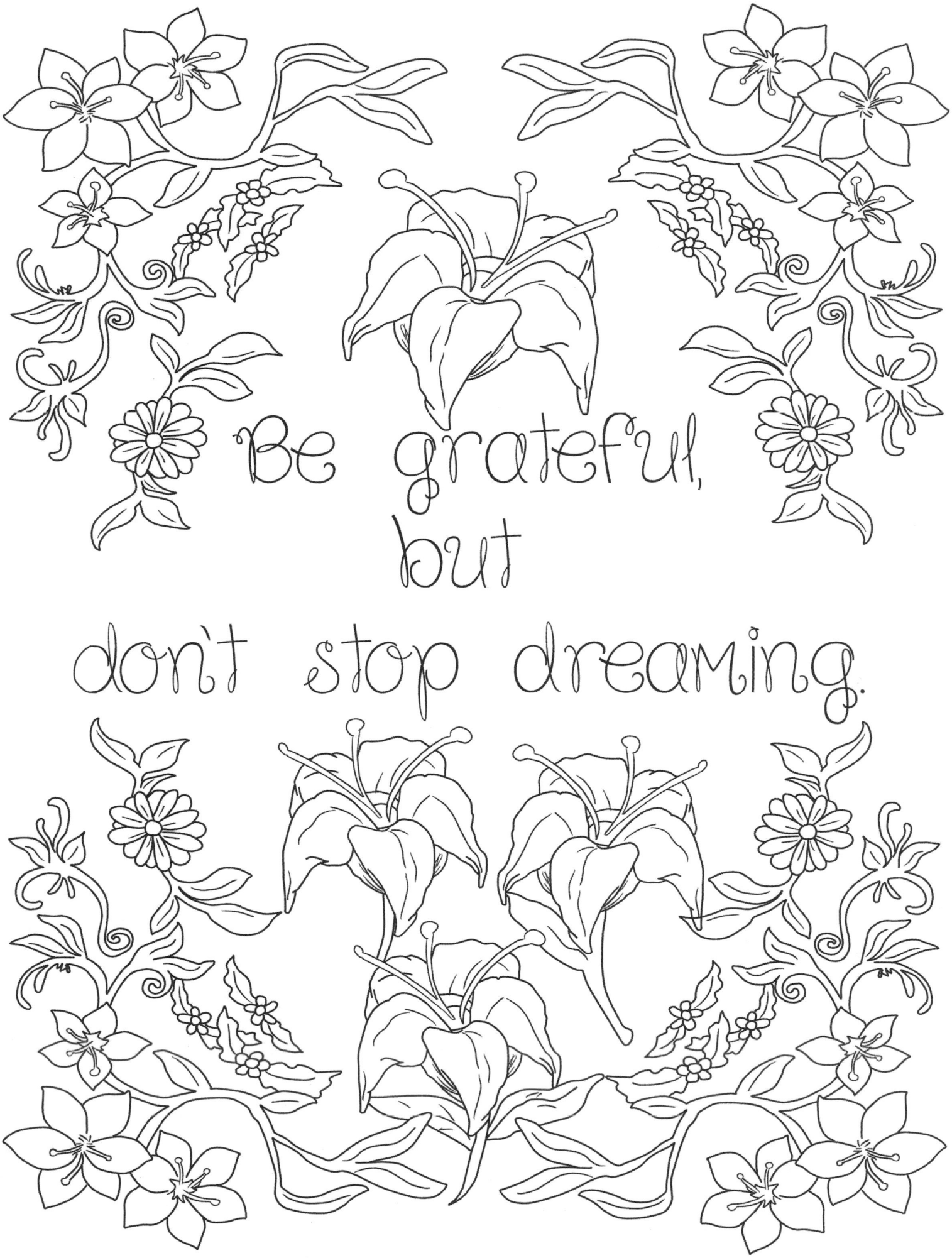
Be grateful,
but
don't stop dreaming.

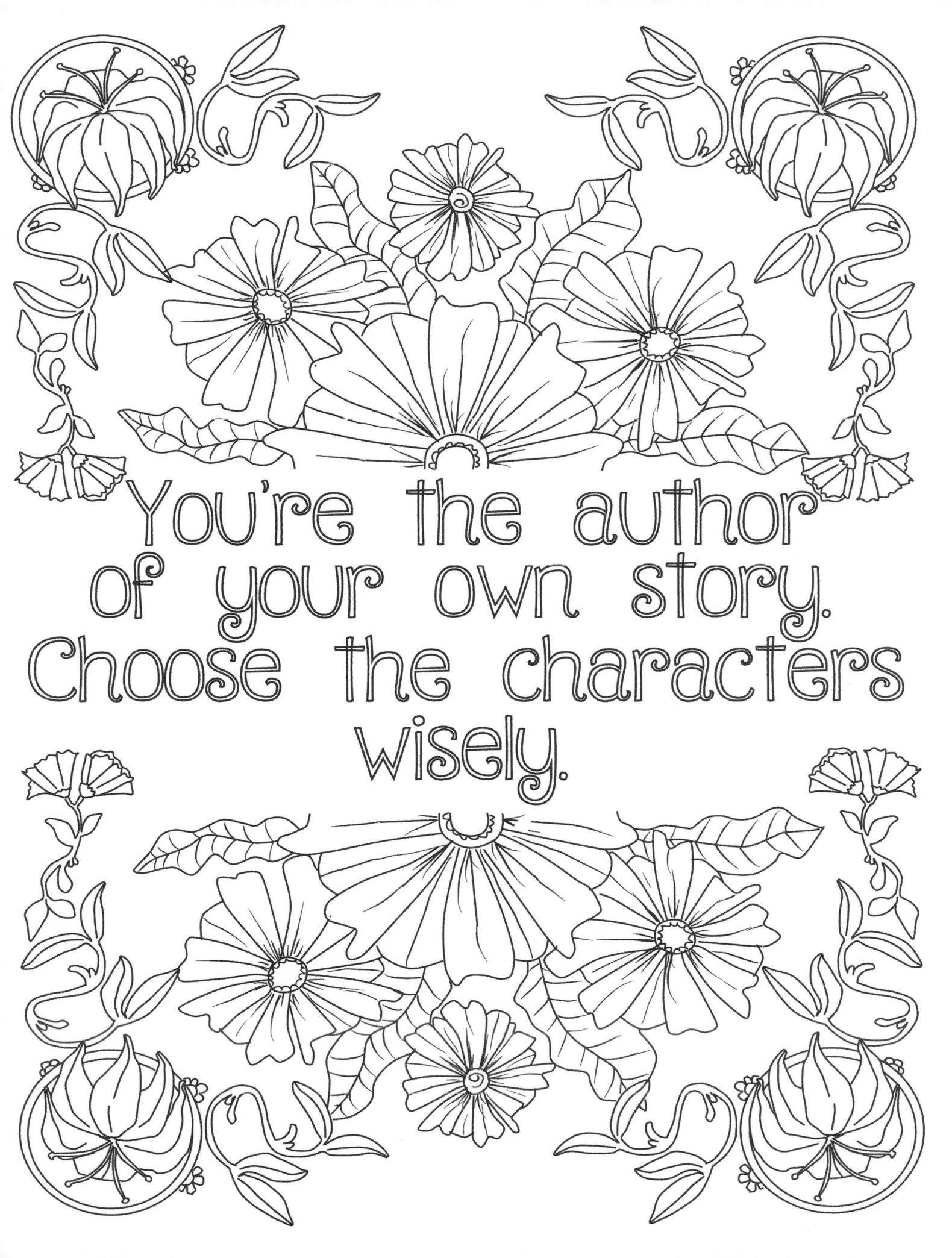
You're the author
of your own story.
Choose the characters
wisely.

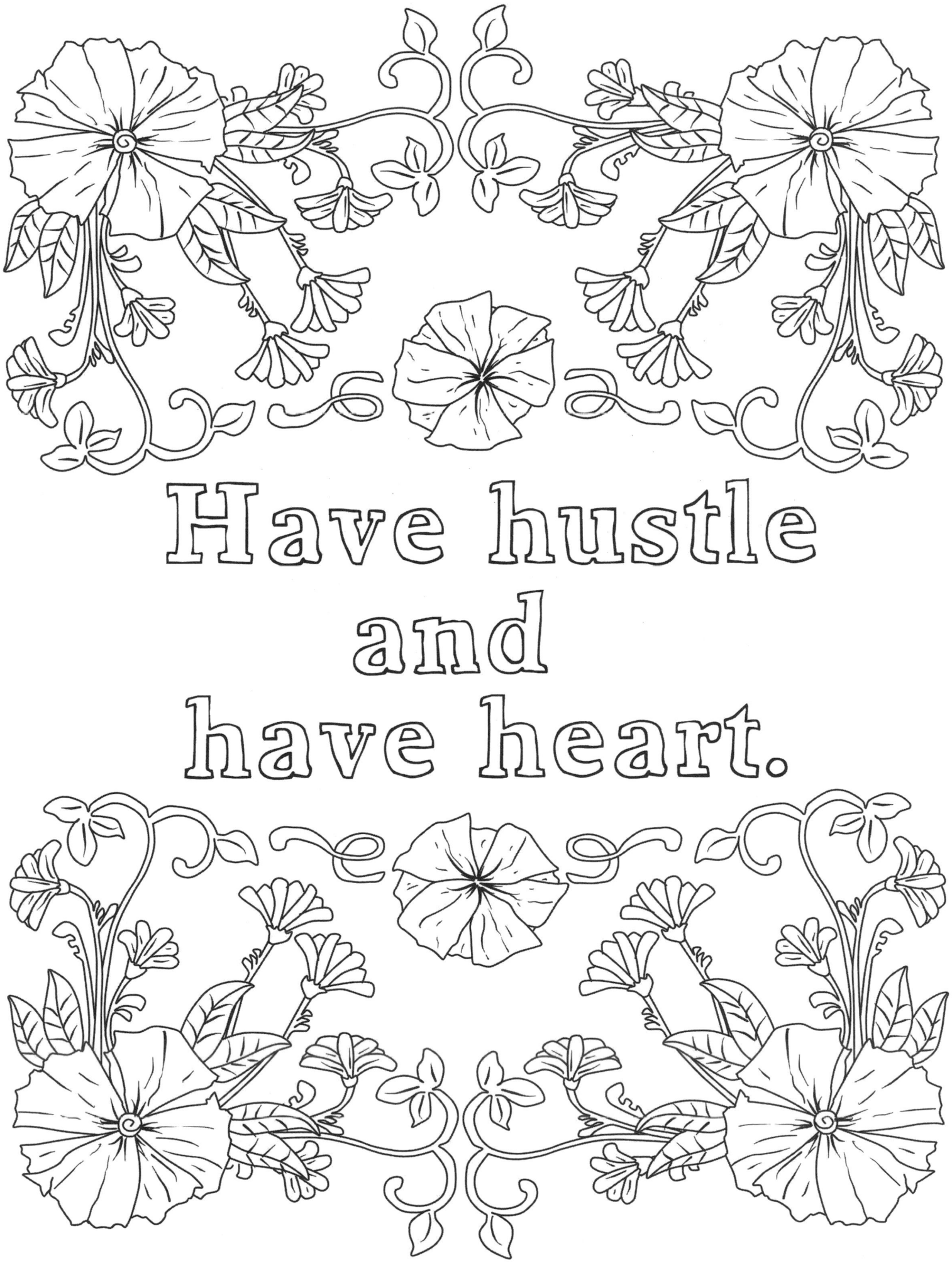
Have hustle
and
have heart.

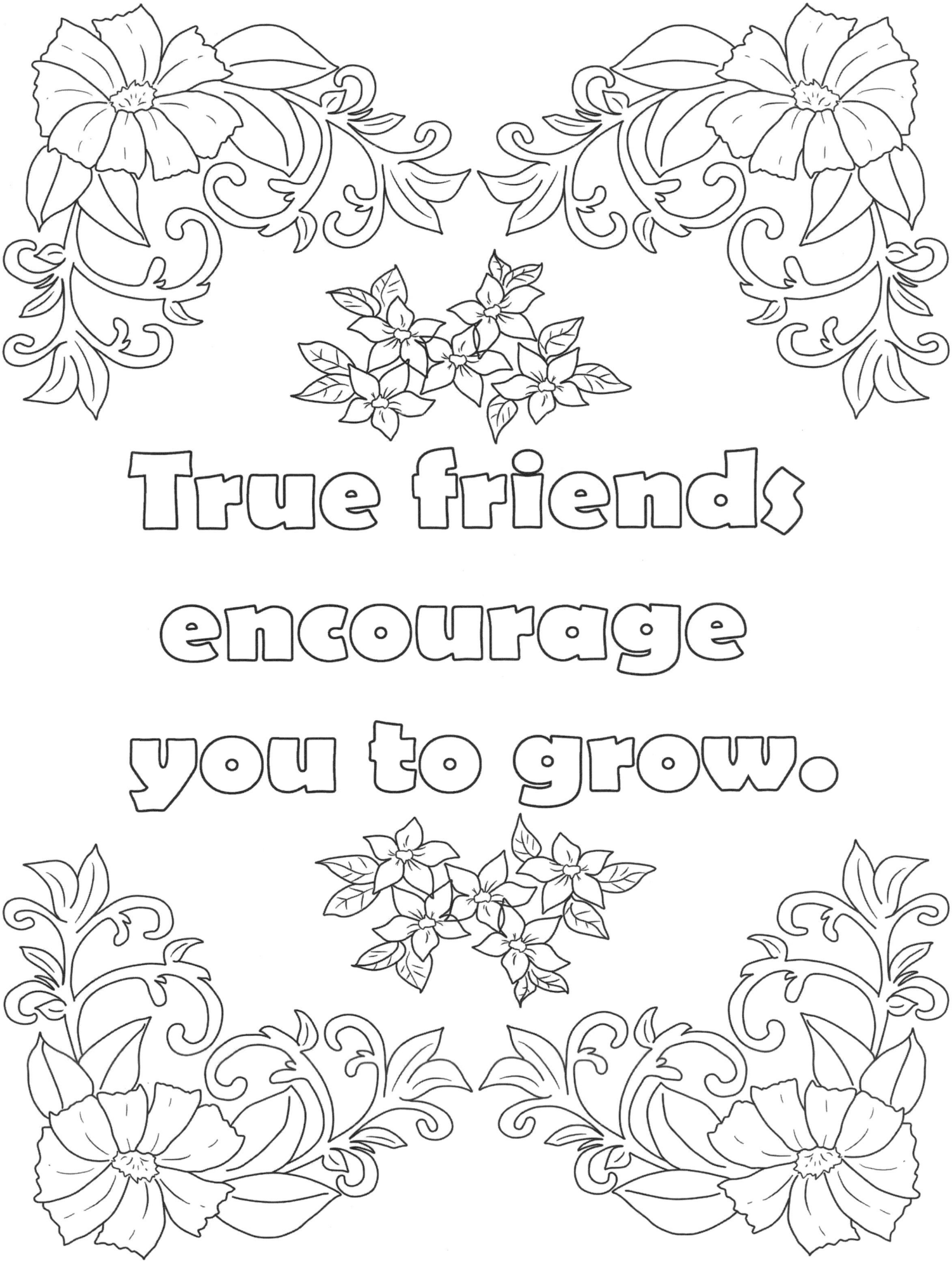
True friends
encourage
you to grow.

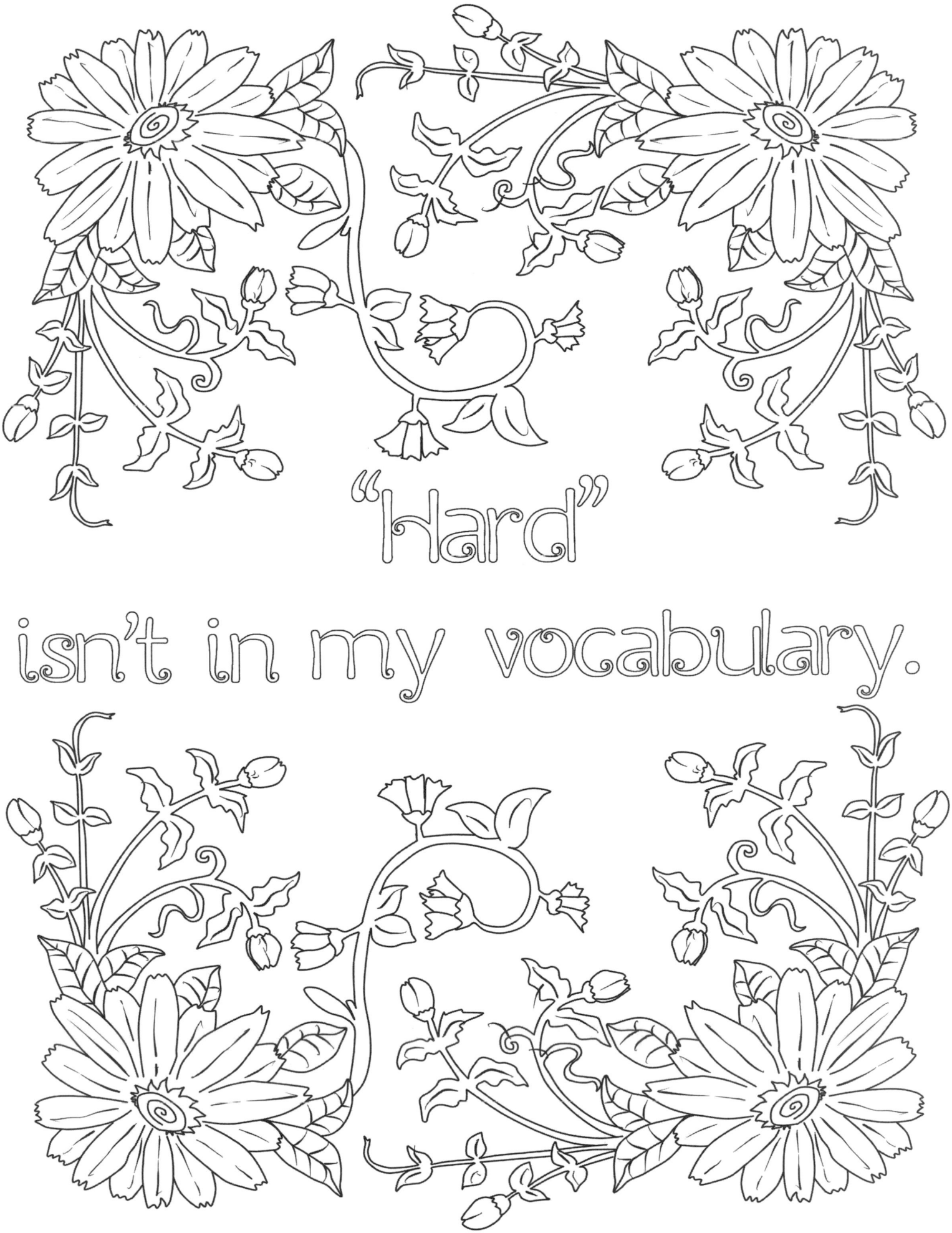
"Hard"
isn't in my vocabulary.

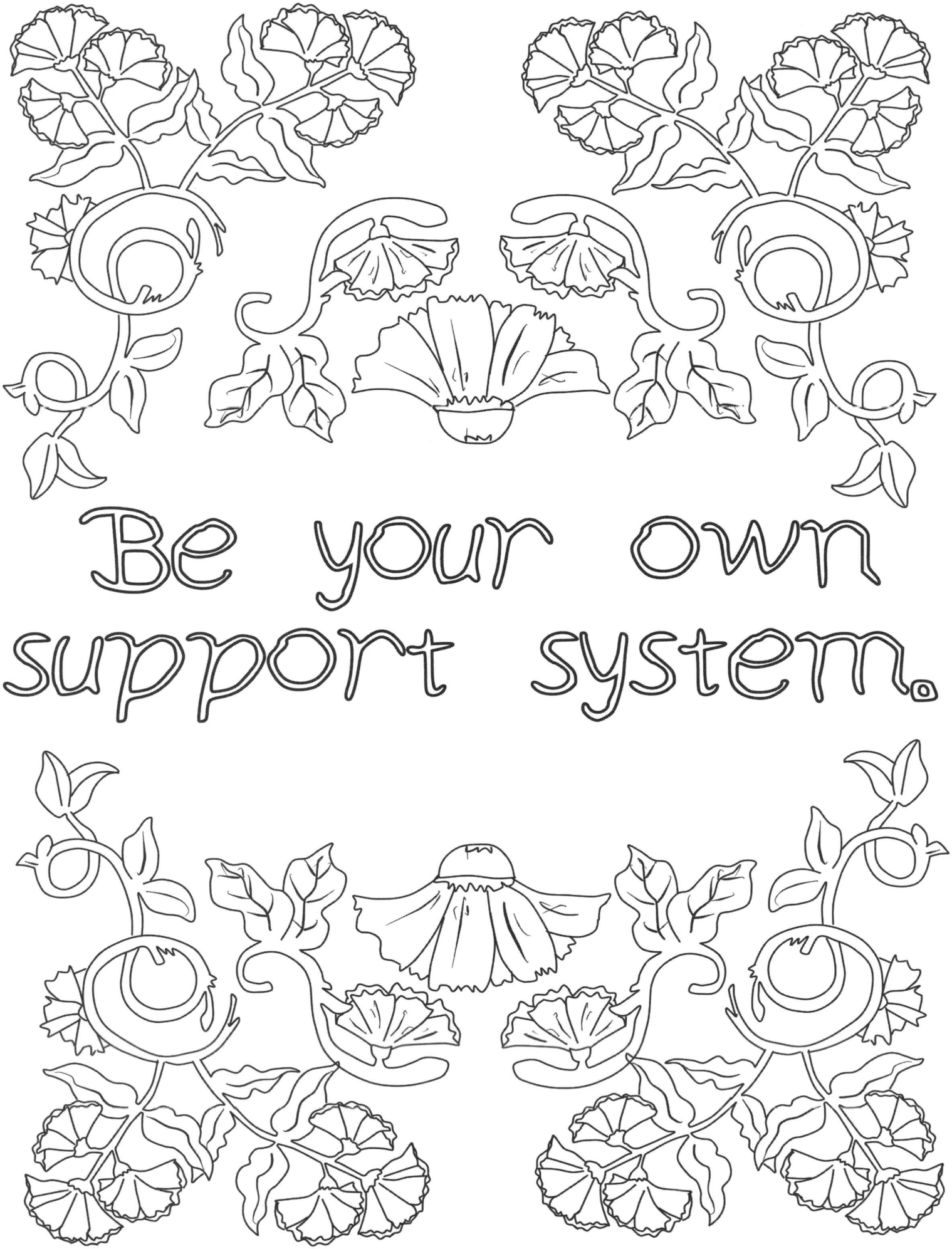
Be your own
support system.

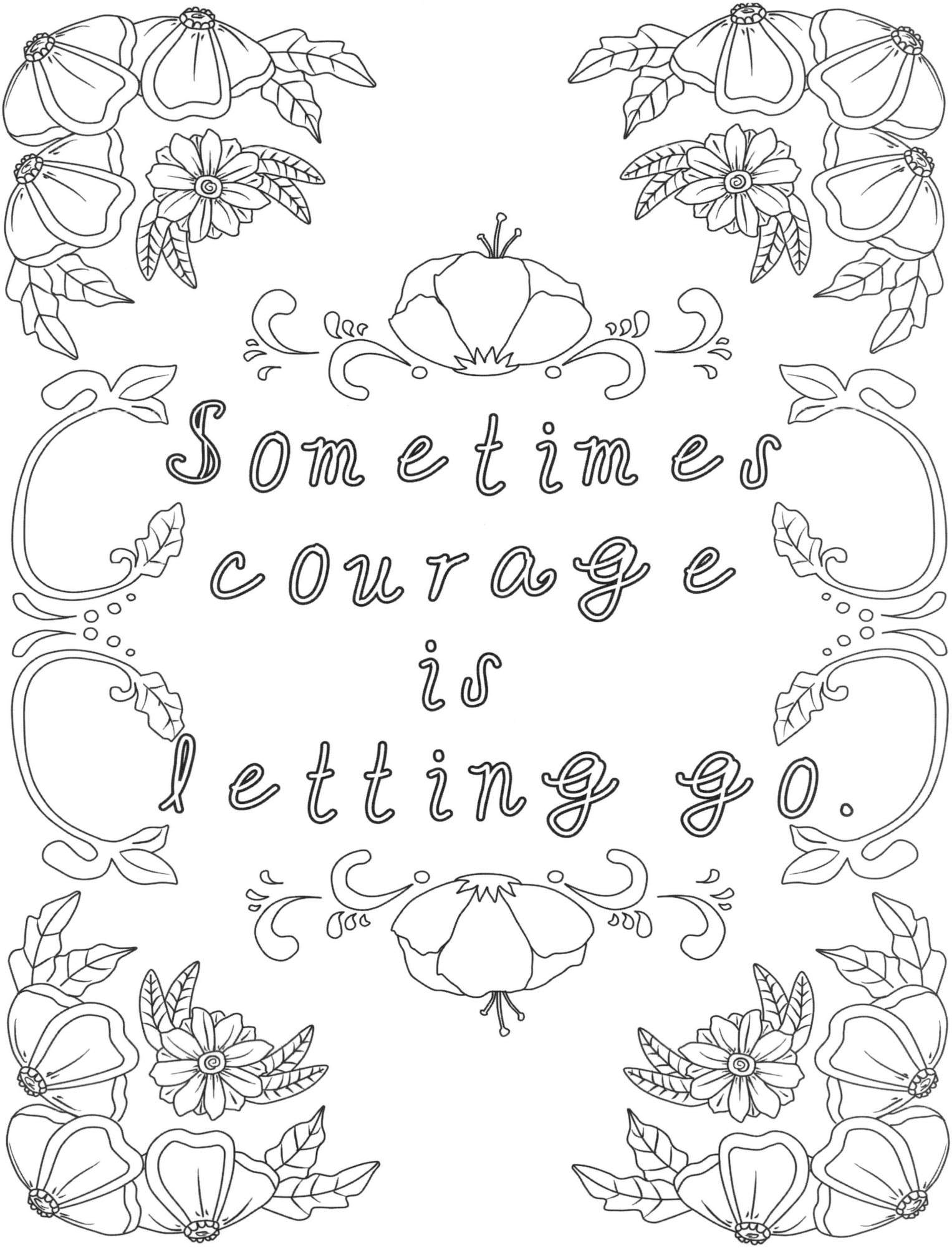
Sometimes
courage
is
letting go.

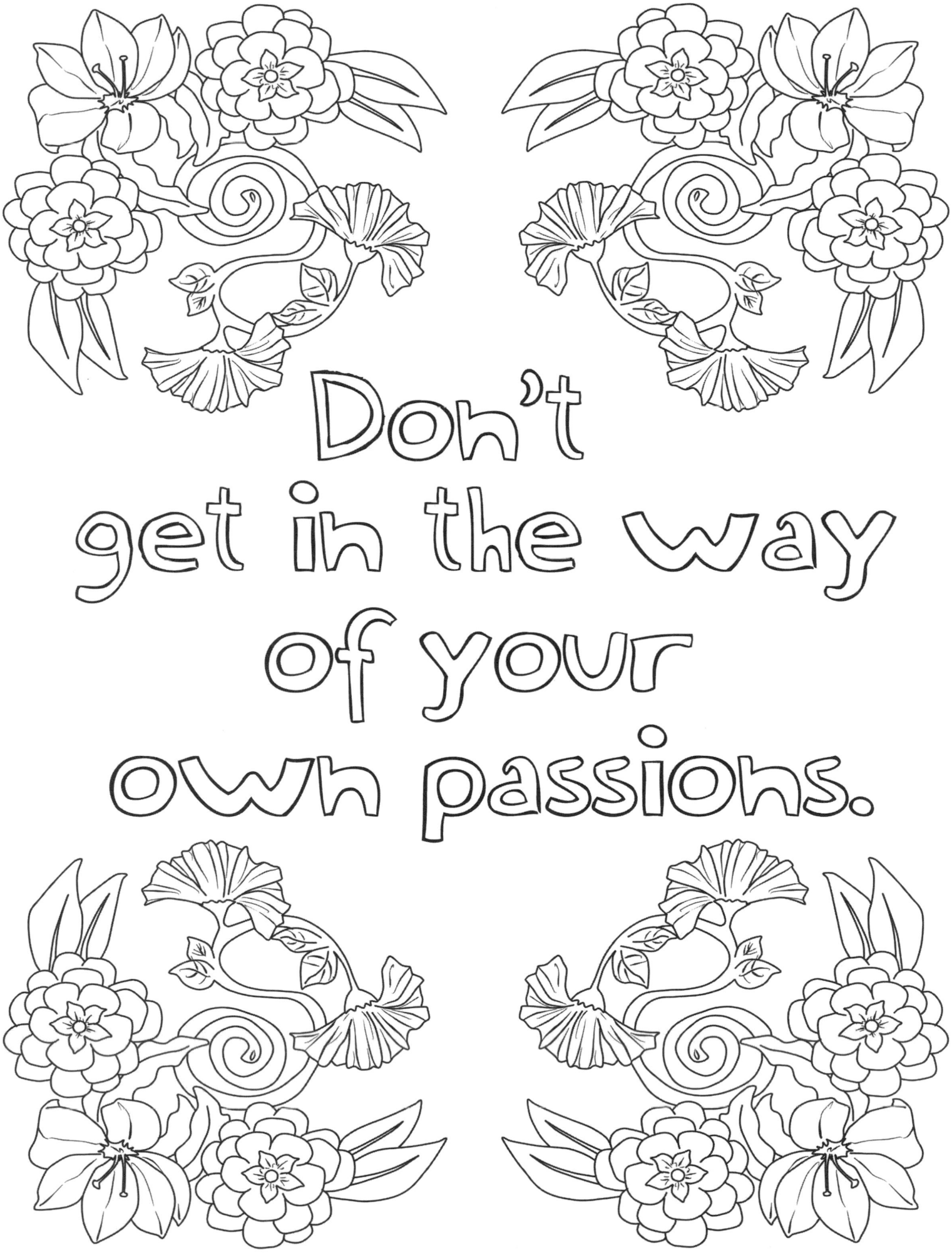
Don't
get in the way
of your
own passions.

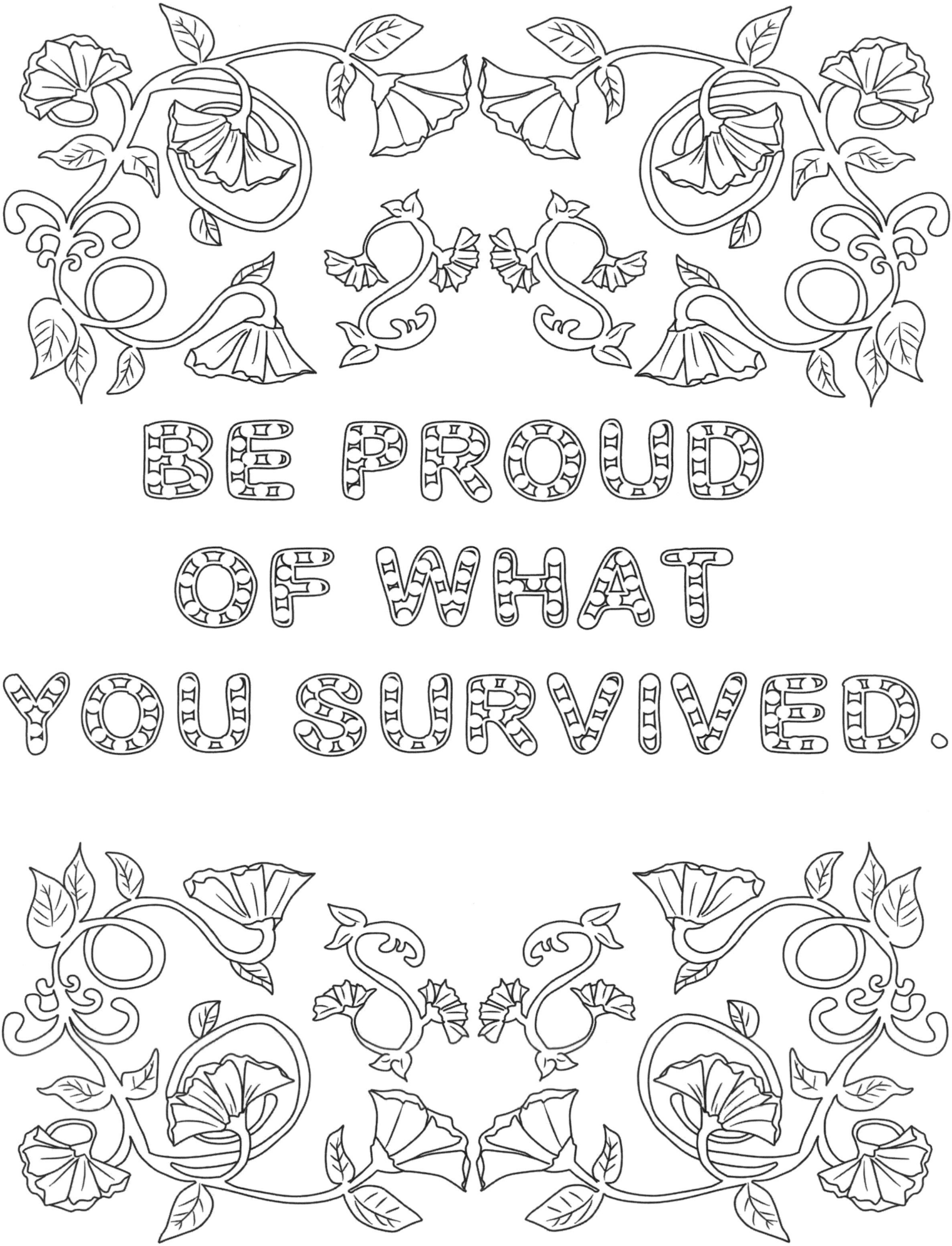
BE PROUD
OF WHAT
YOU SURVIVED.

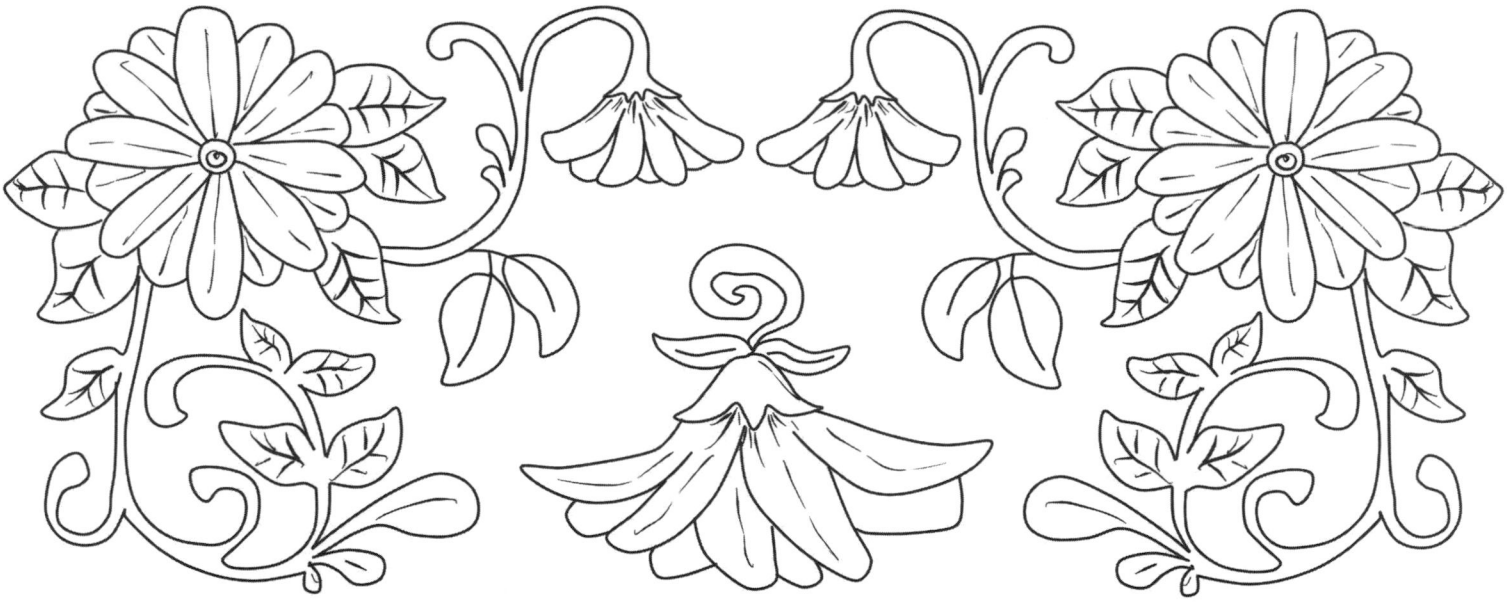

DON'T FEAR
THE FUTURE.

IT'S GOING TO
HAPPEN ANYWAY.

THE KINDNESS
OF STRANGERS
IS AN AMAZING THING.

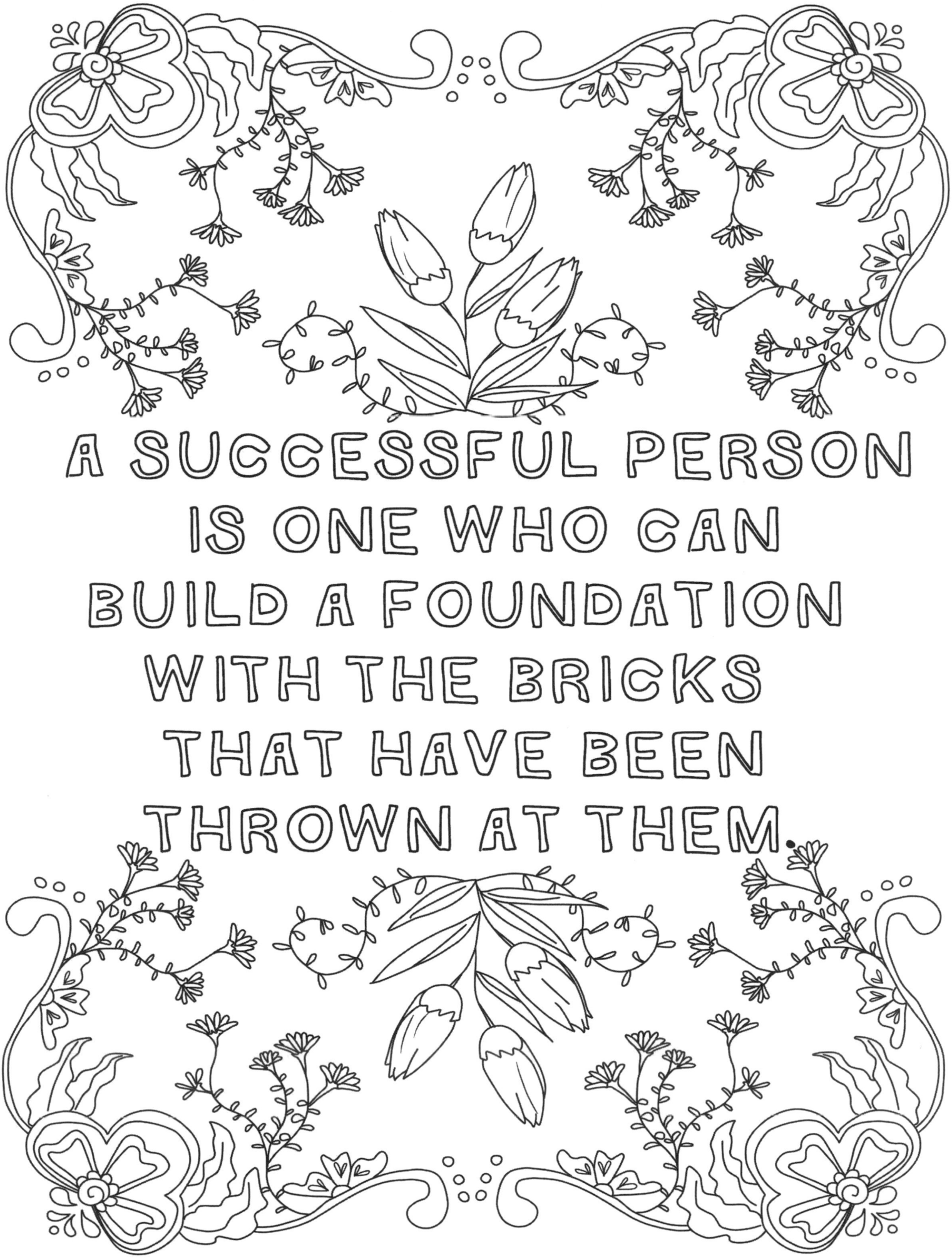
A SUCCESSFUL PERSON
IS ONE WHO CAN
BUILD A FOUNDATION
WITH THE BRICKS
THAT HAVE BEEN
THROWN AT THEM.

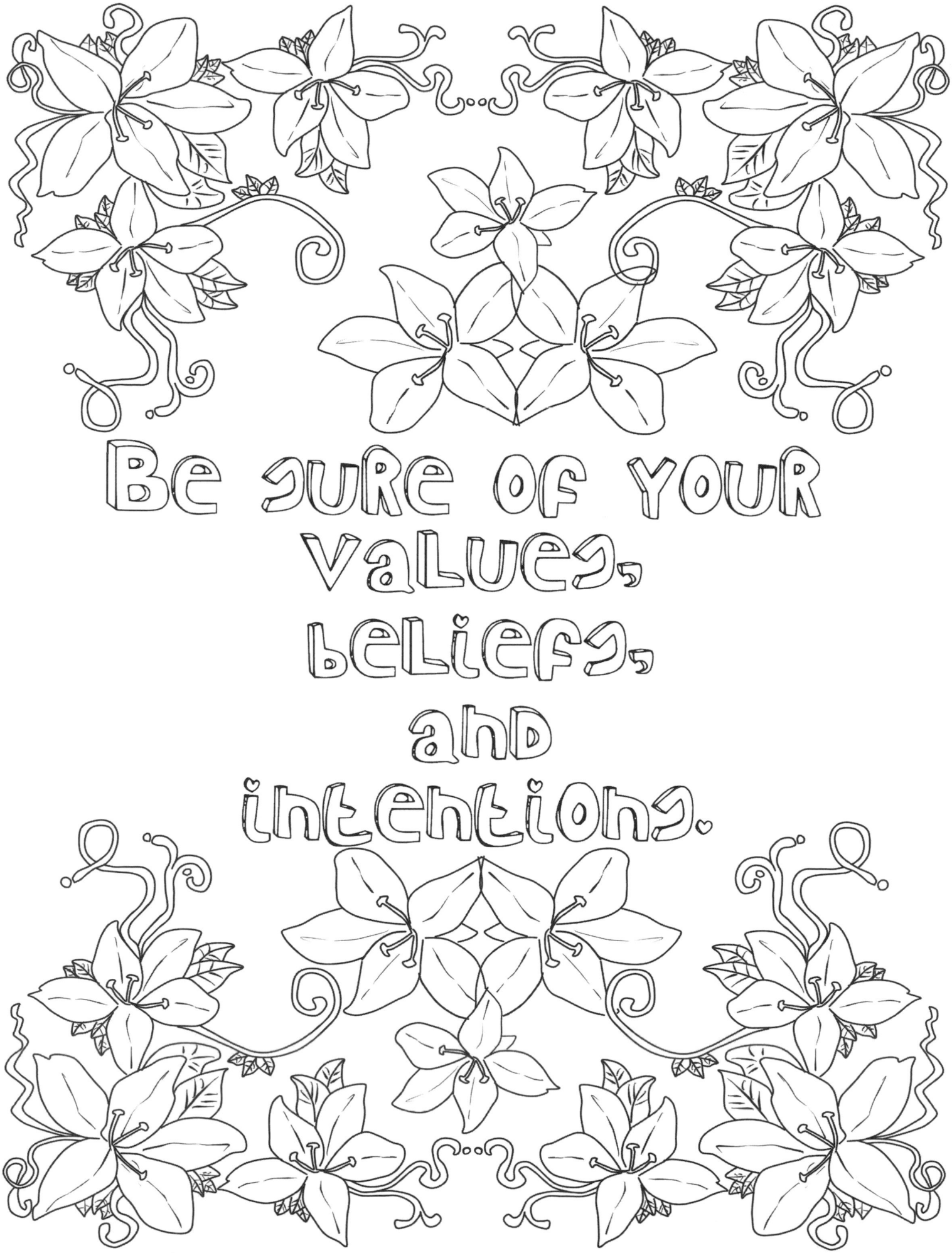
Be sure of your values, beliefs, and intentions.

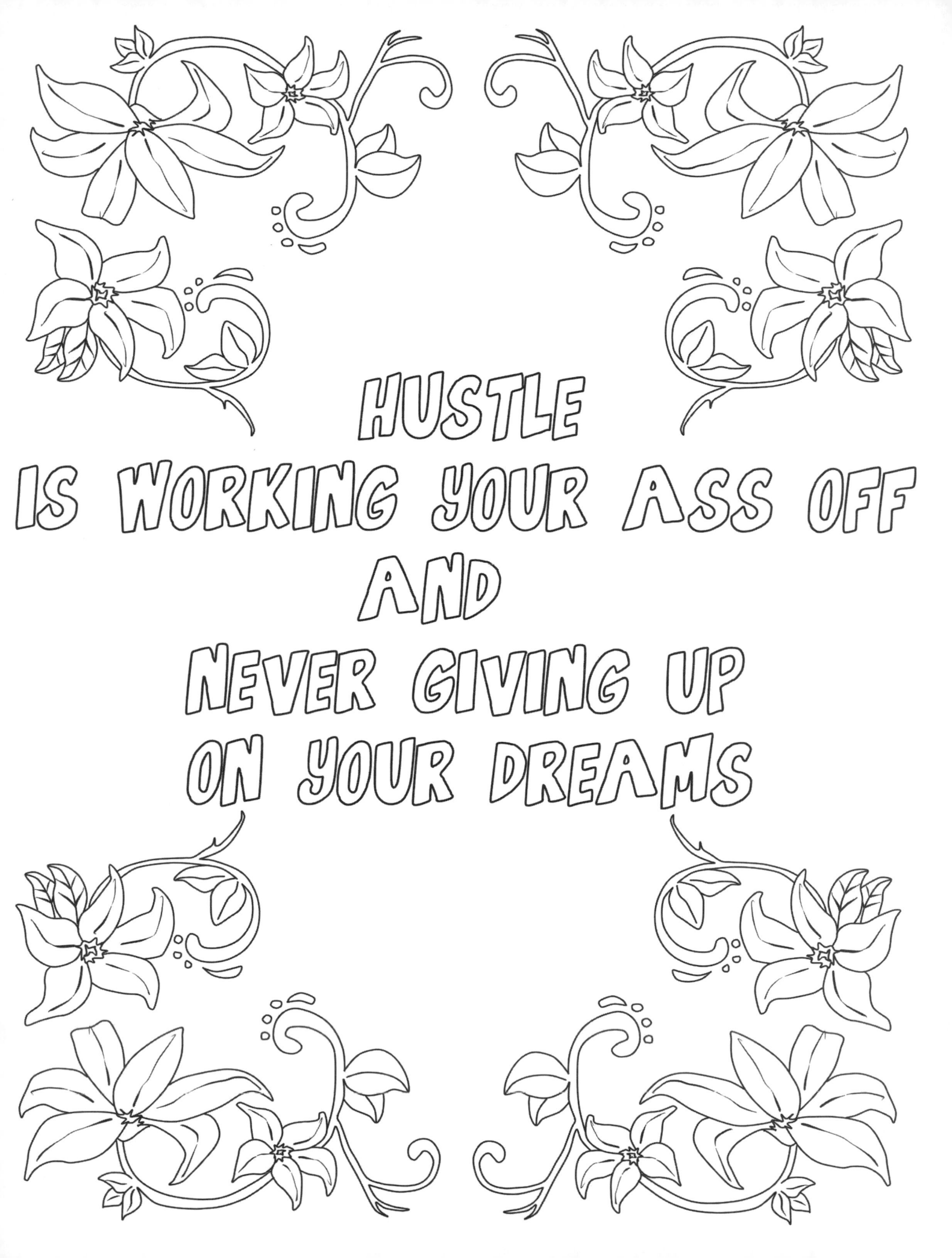
HUSTLE
IS WORKING YOUR ASS OFF
AND
NEVER GIVING UP
ON YOUR DREAMS

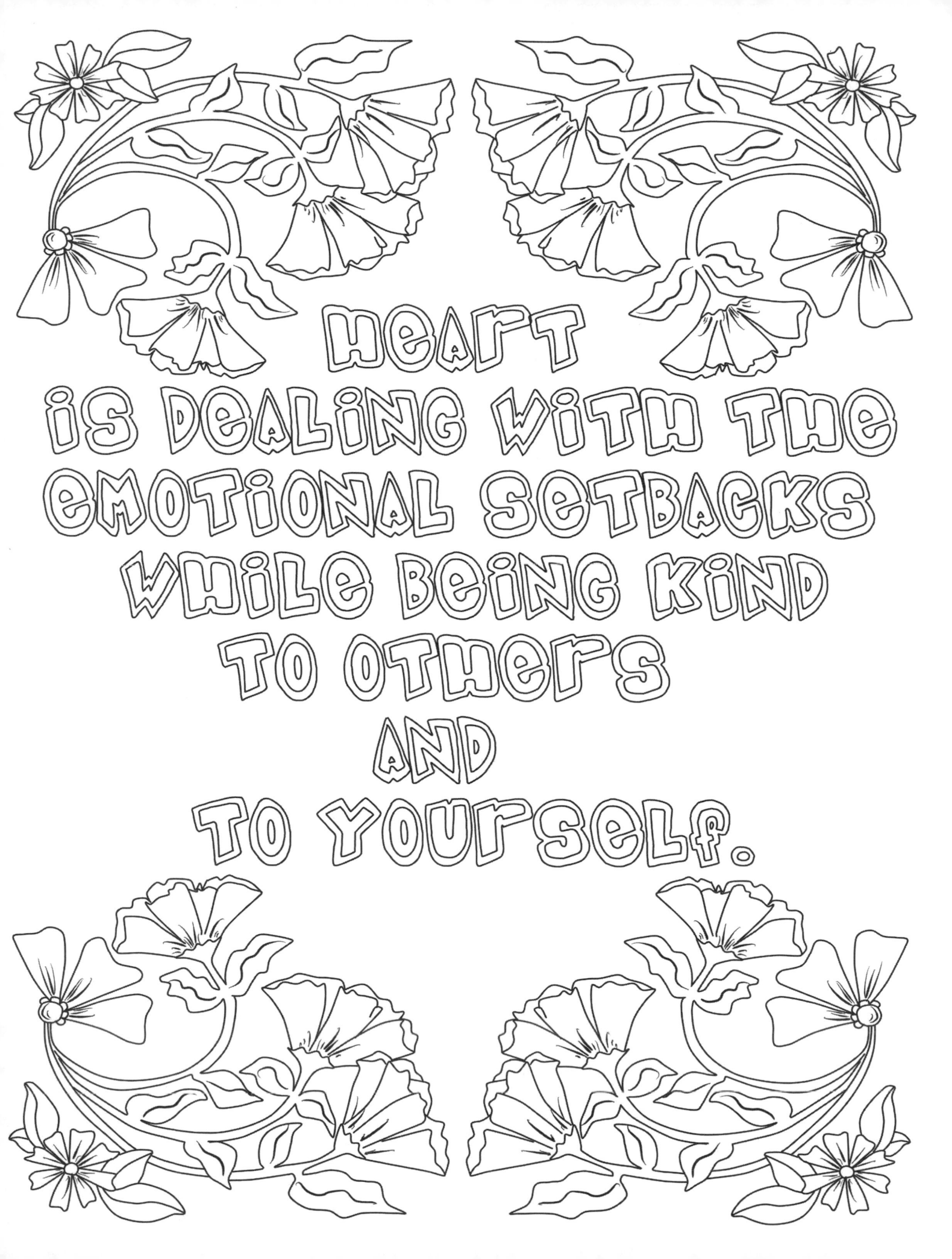
HEART
IS DEALING WITH THE
EMOTIONAL SETBACKS
WHILE BEING KIND
TO OTHERS
AND
TO YOURSELF.

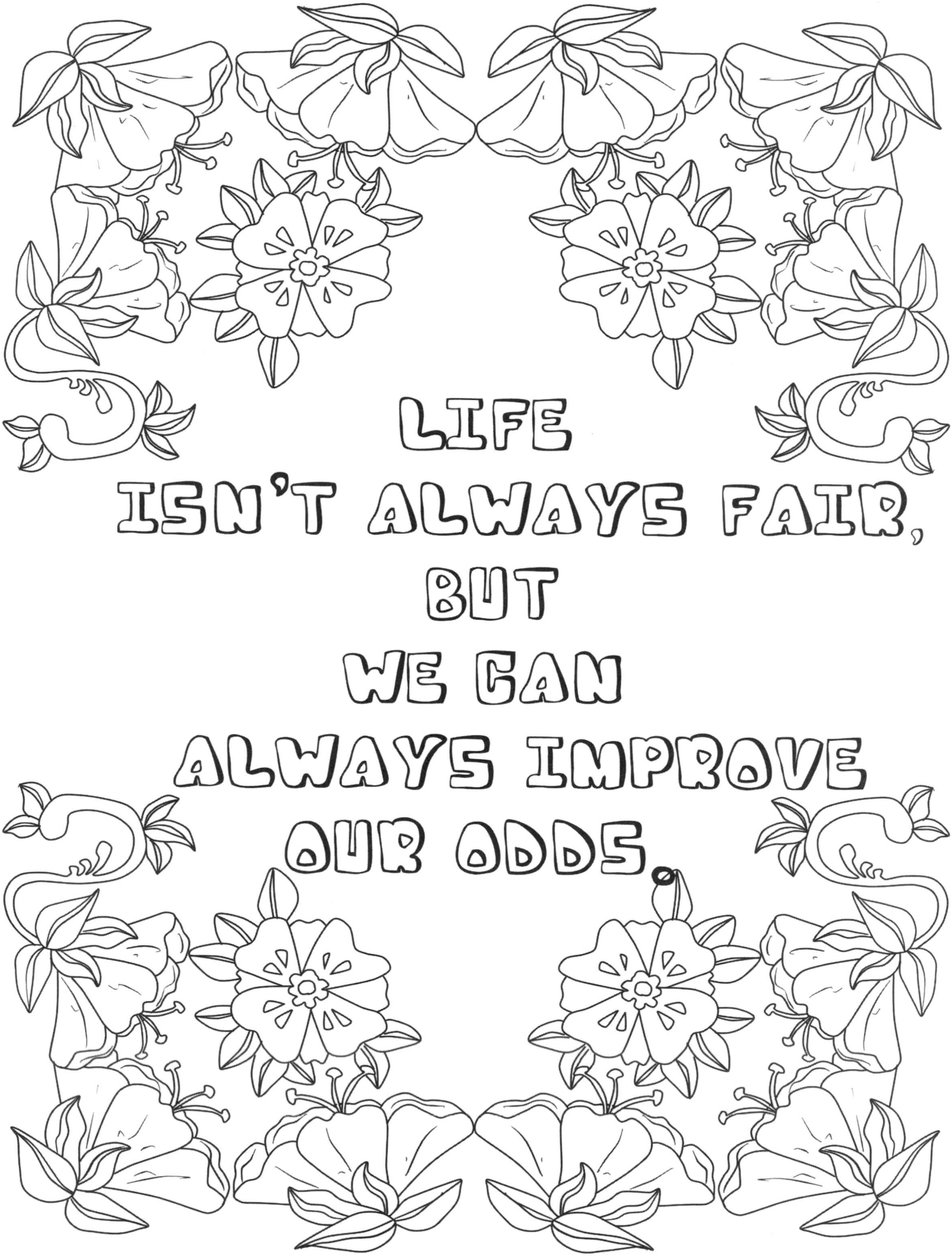
LIFE
ISN'T ALWAYS FAIR,
BUT
WE CAN
ALWAYS IMPROVE
OUR ODDS.

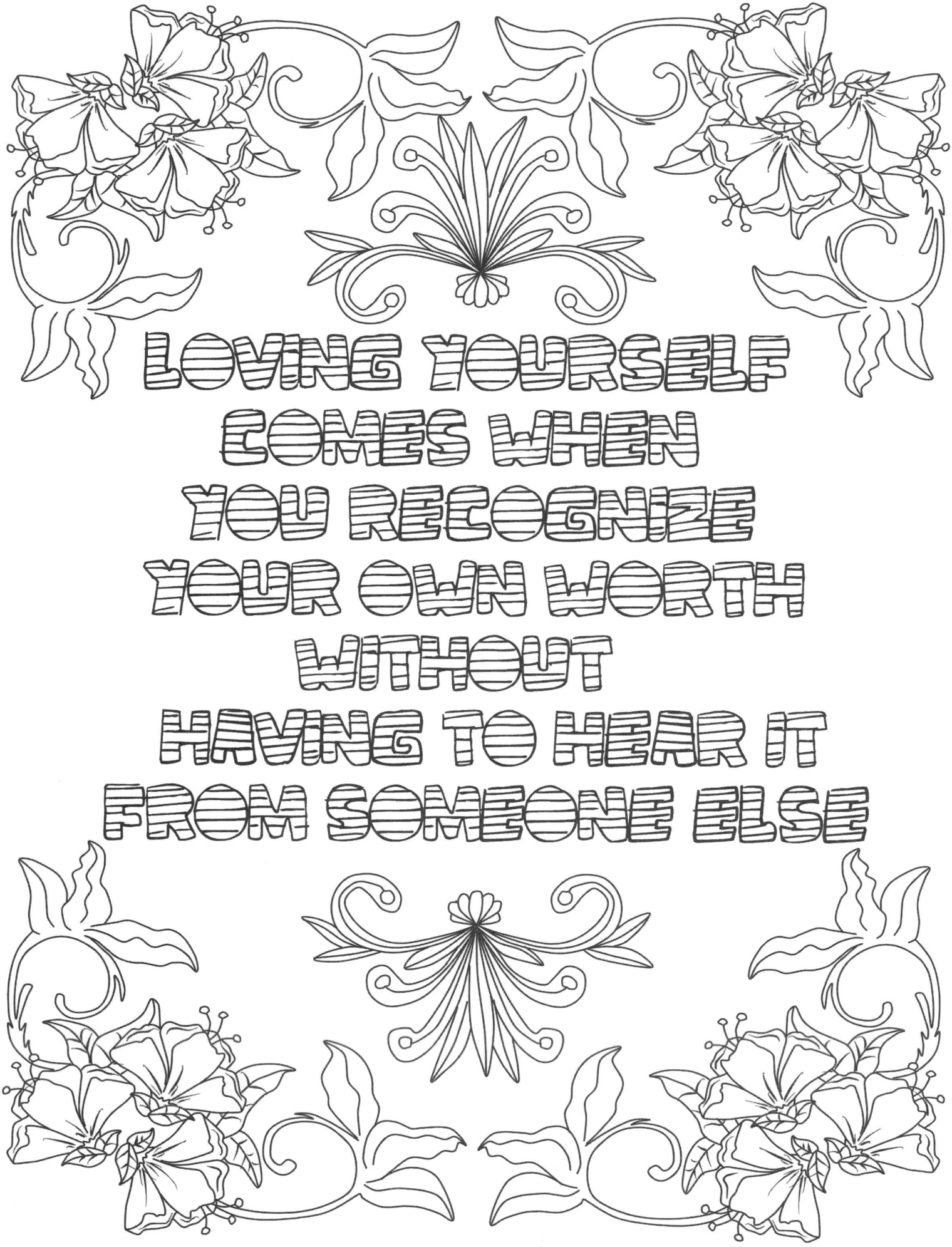
LOVING YOURSELF
COMES WHEN
YOU RECOGNIZE
YOUR OWN WORTH
WITHOUT
HAVING TO HEAR IT
FROM SOMEONE ELSE

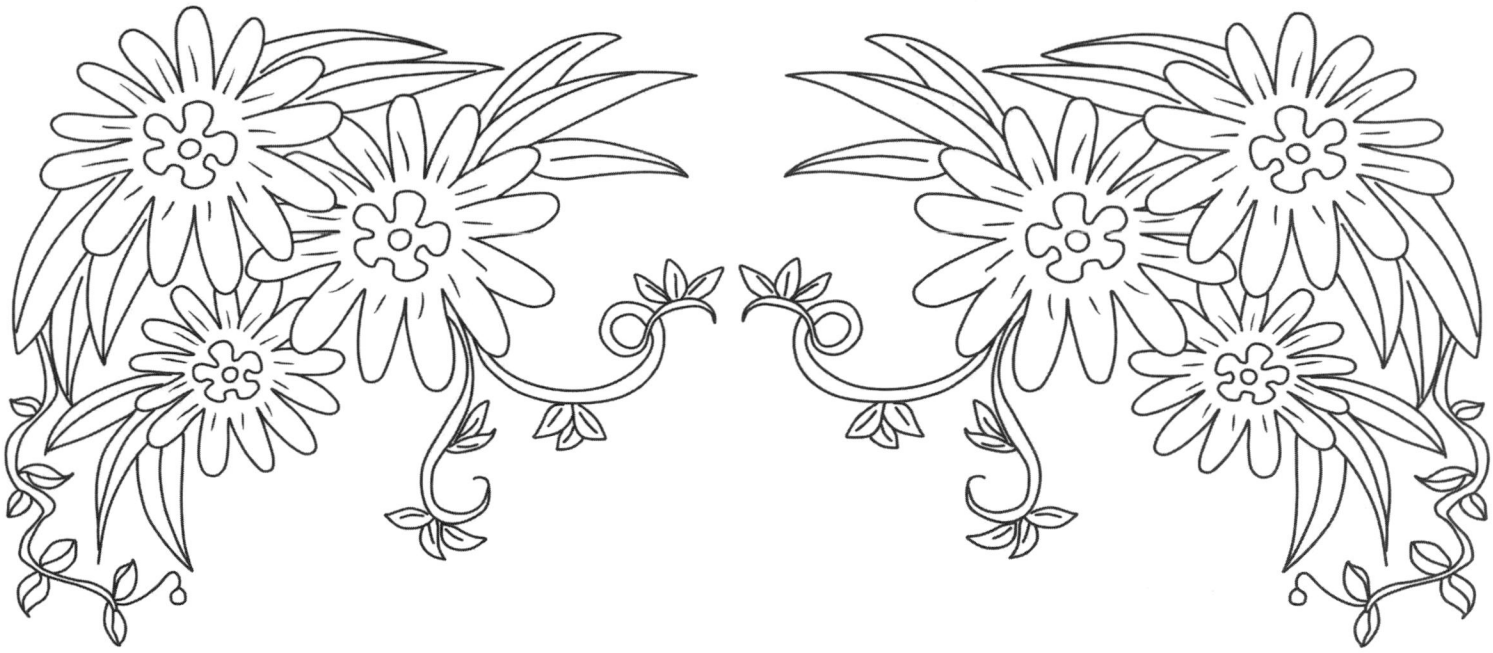

Pleasure and pain come naturally.

Gratitude takes practice.

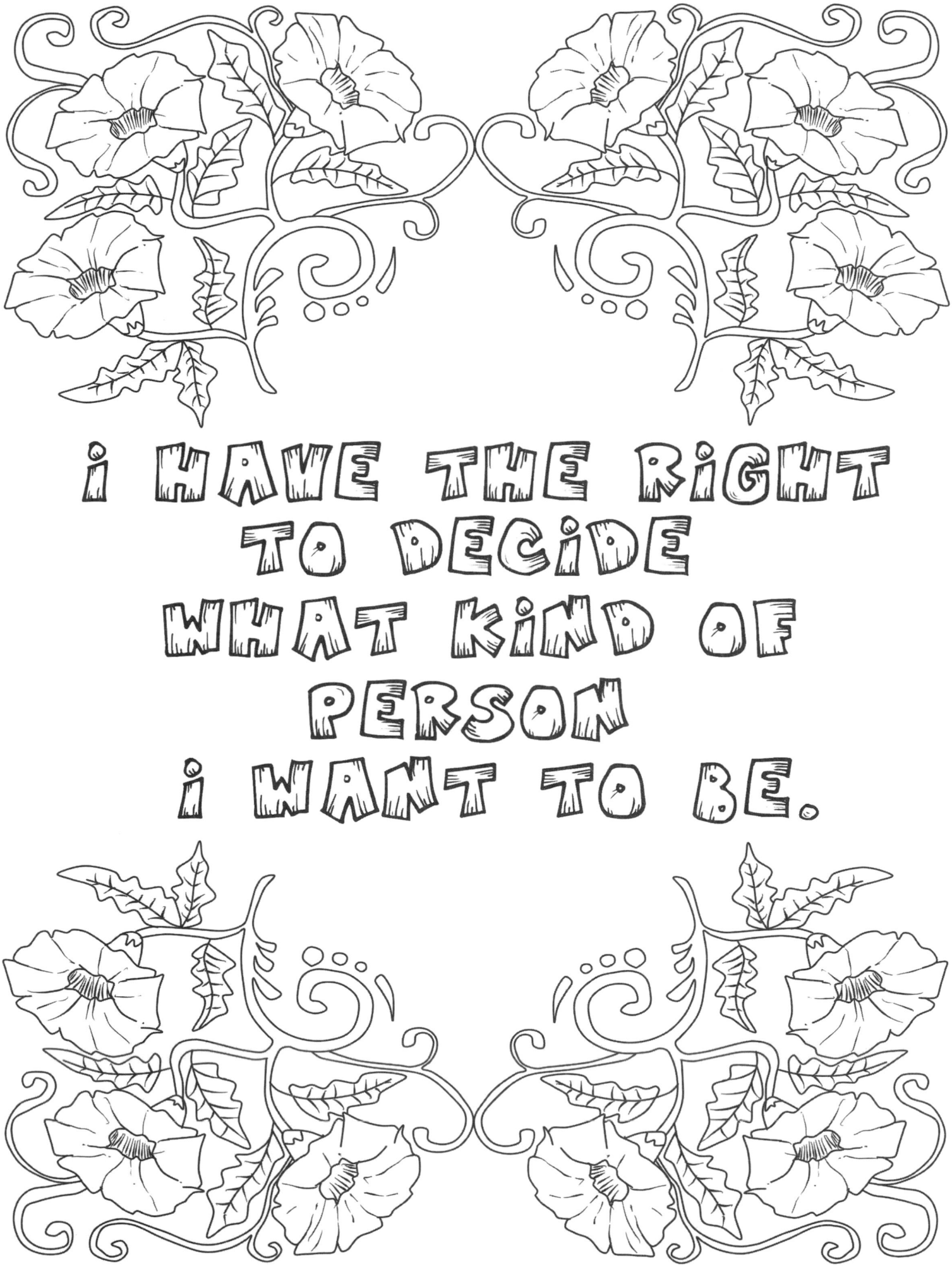
I HAVE THE RIGHT
TO DECIDE
WHAT KIND OF
PERSON
I WANT TO BE.

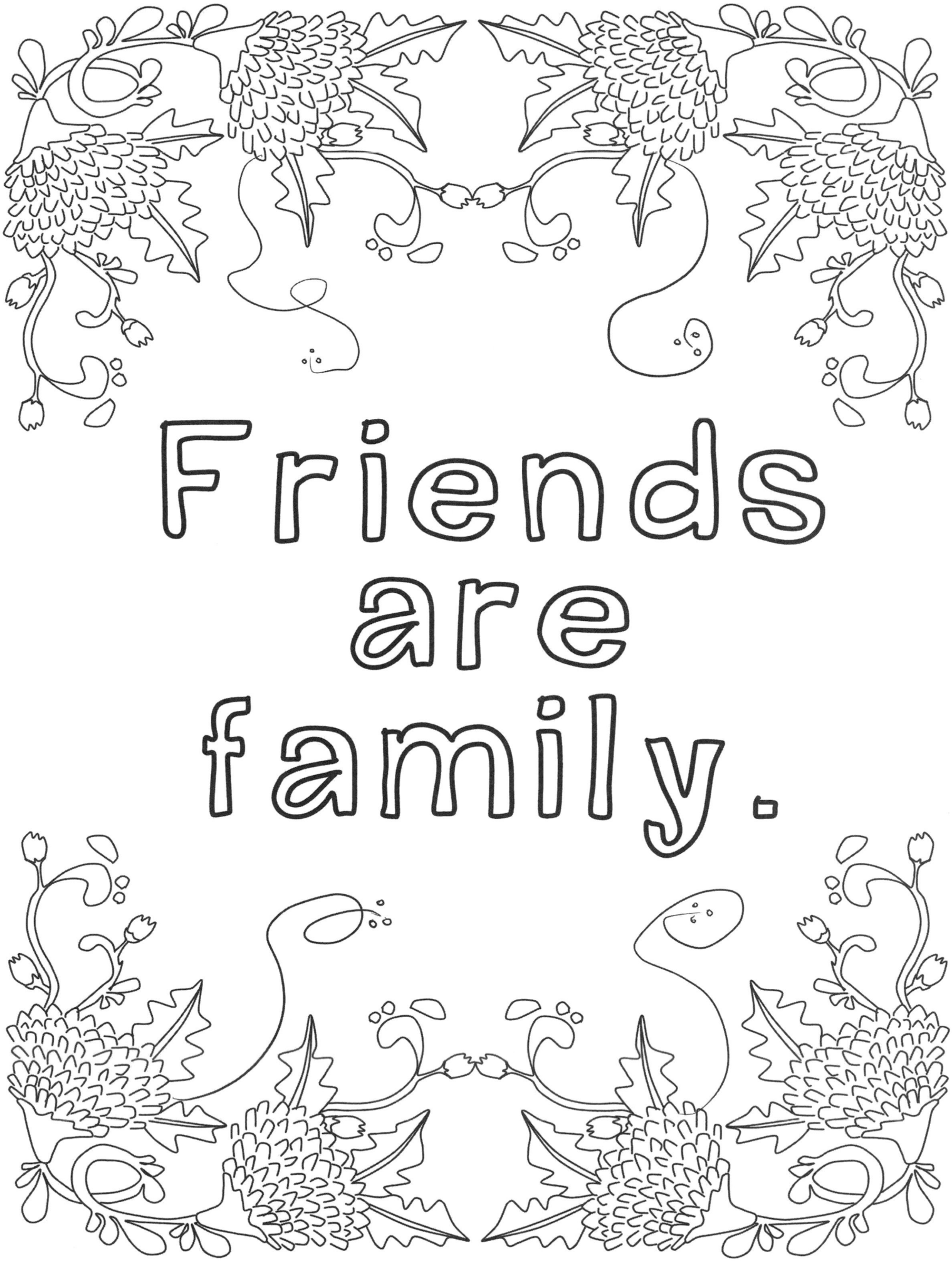
Friends
are
family.

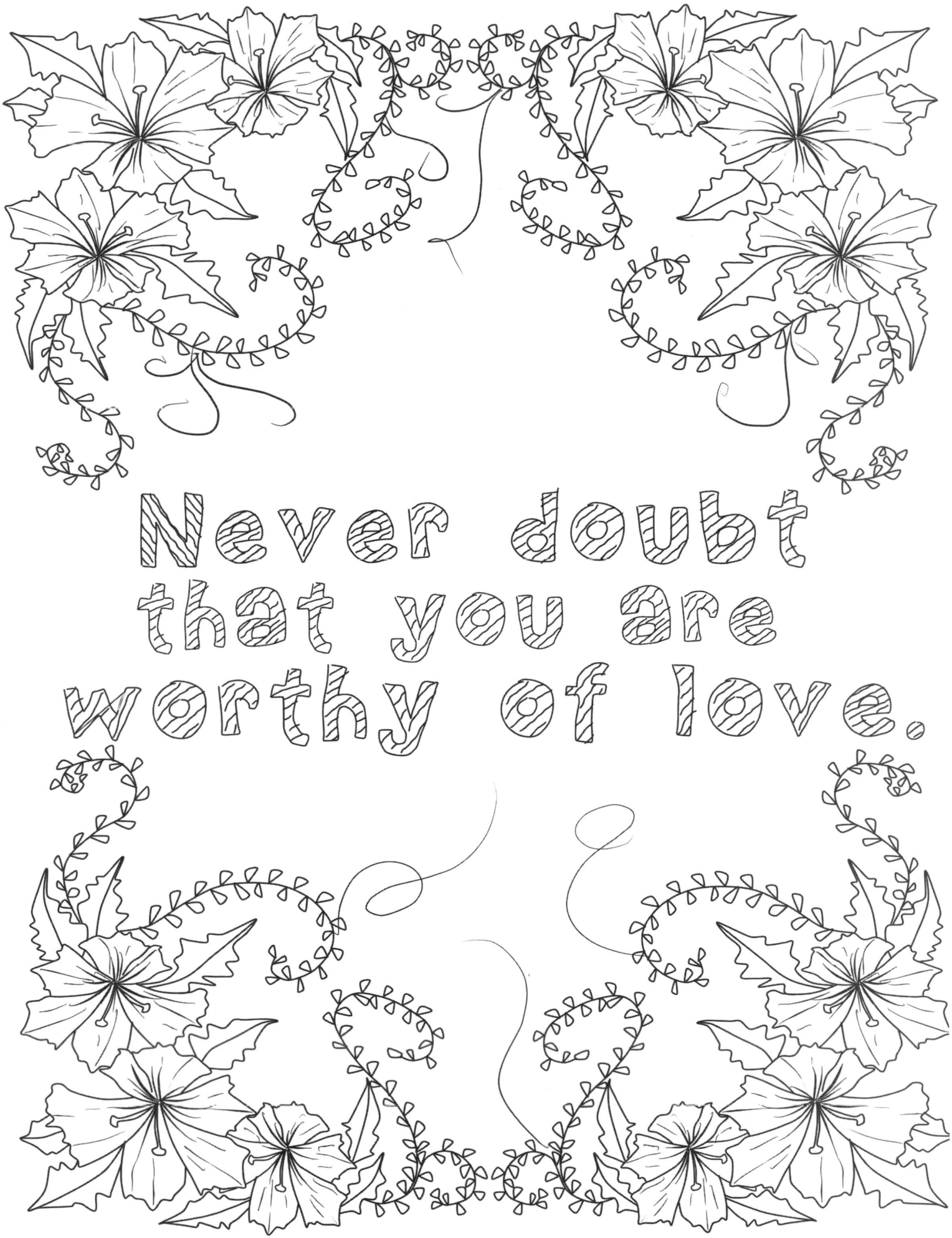
Never doubt
that you are
worthy of love.

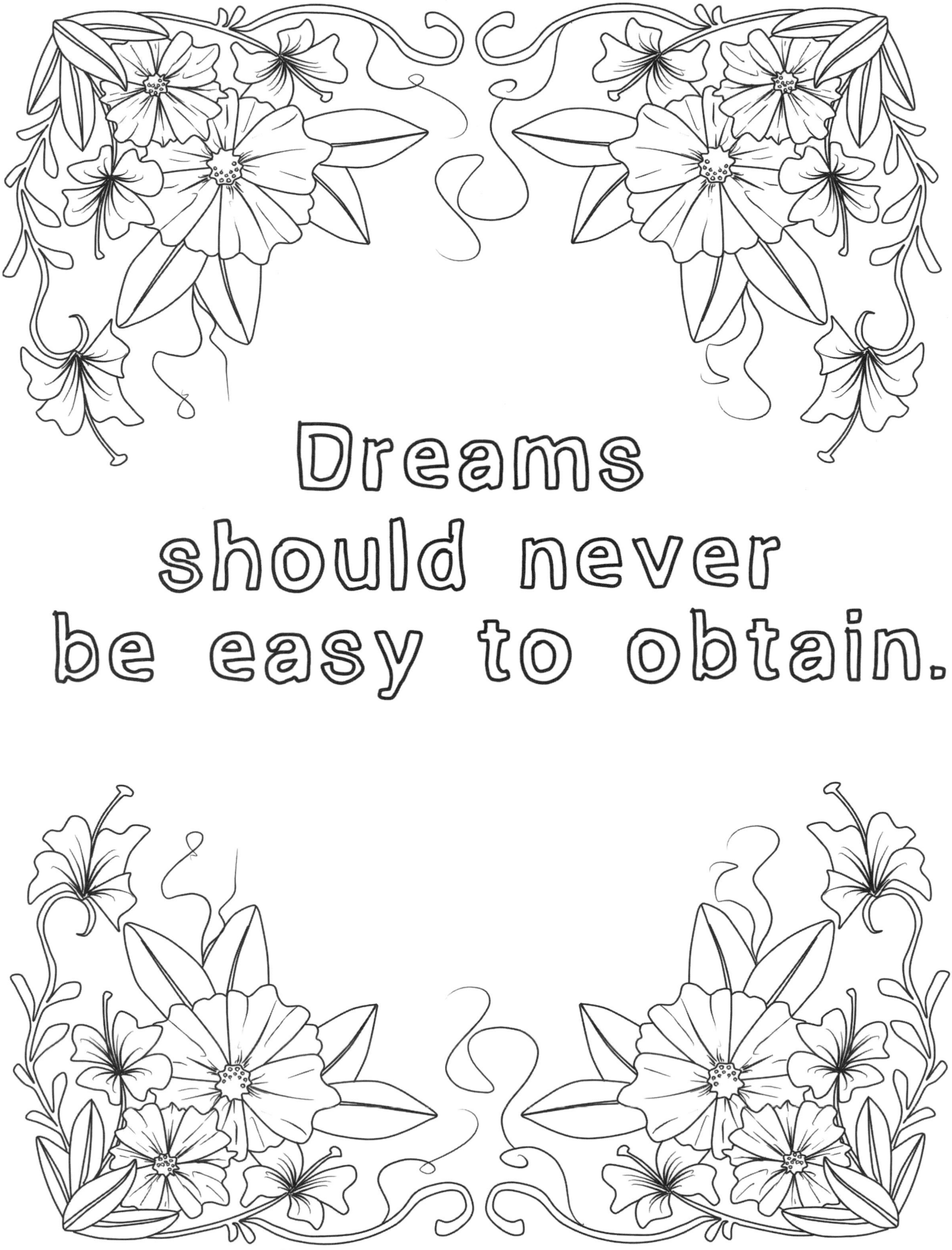
Dreams
should never
be easy to obtain.

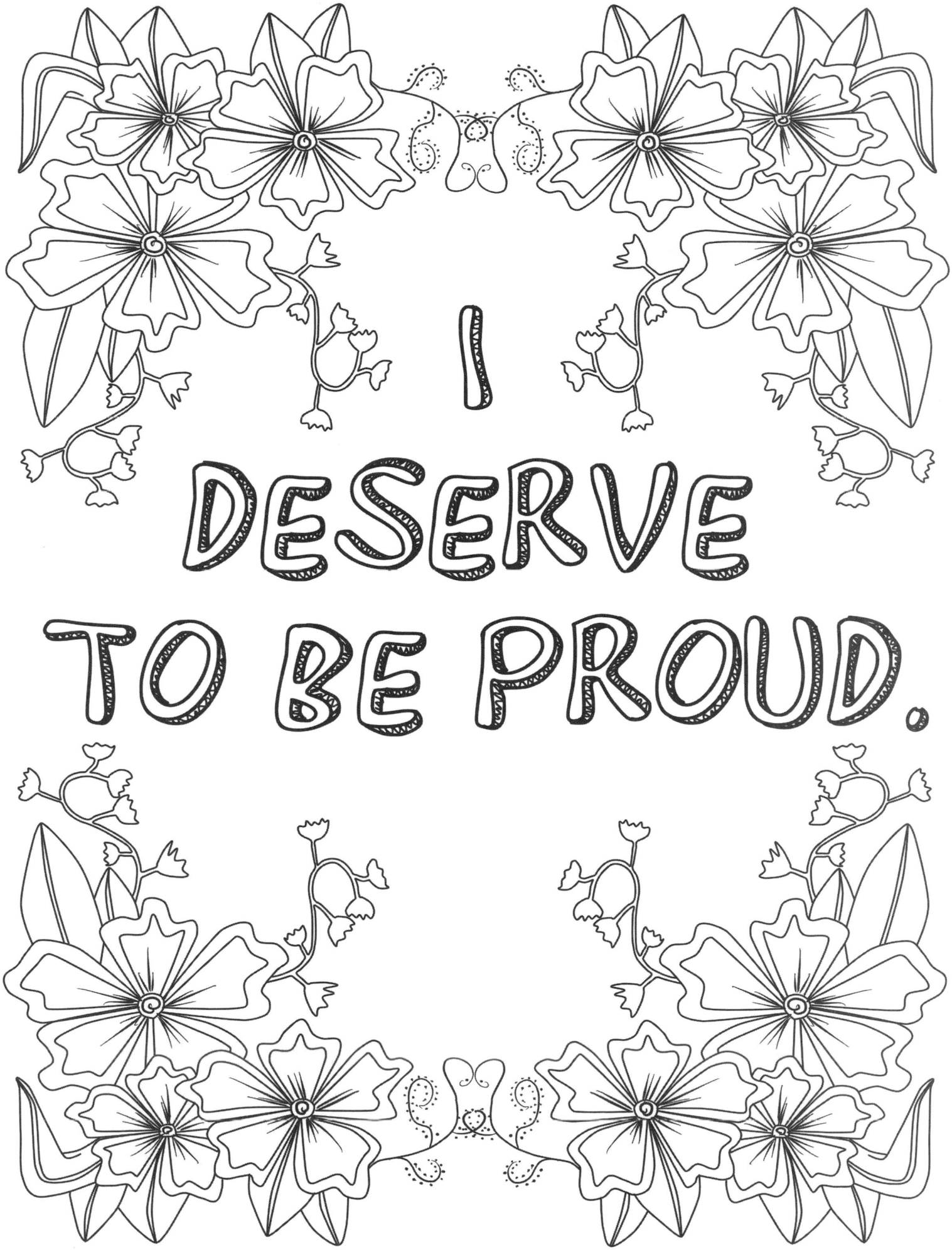
I
DESERVE
TO BE PROUD.

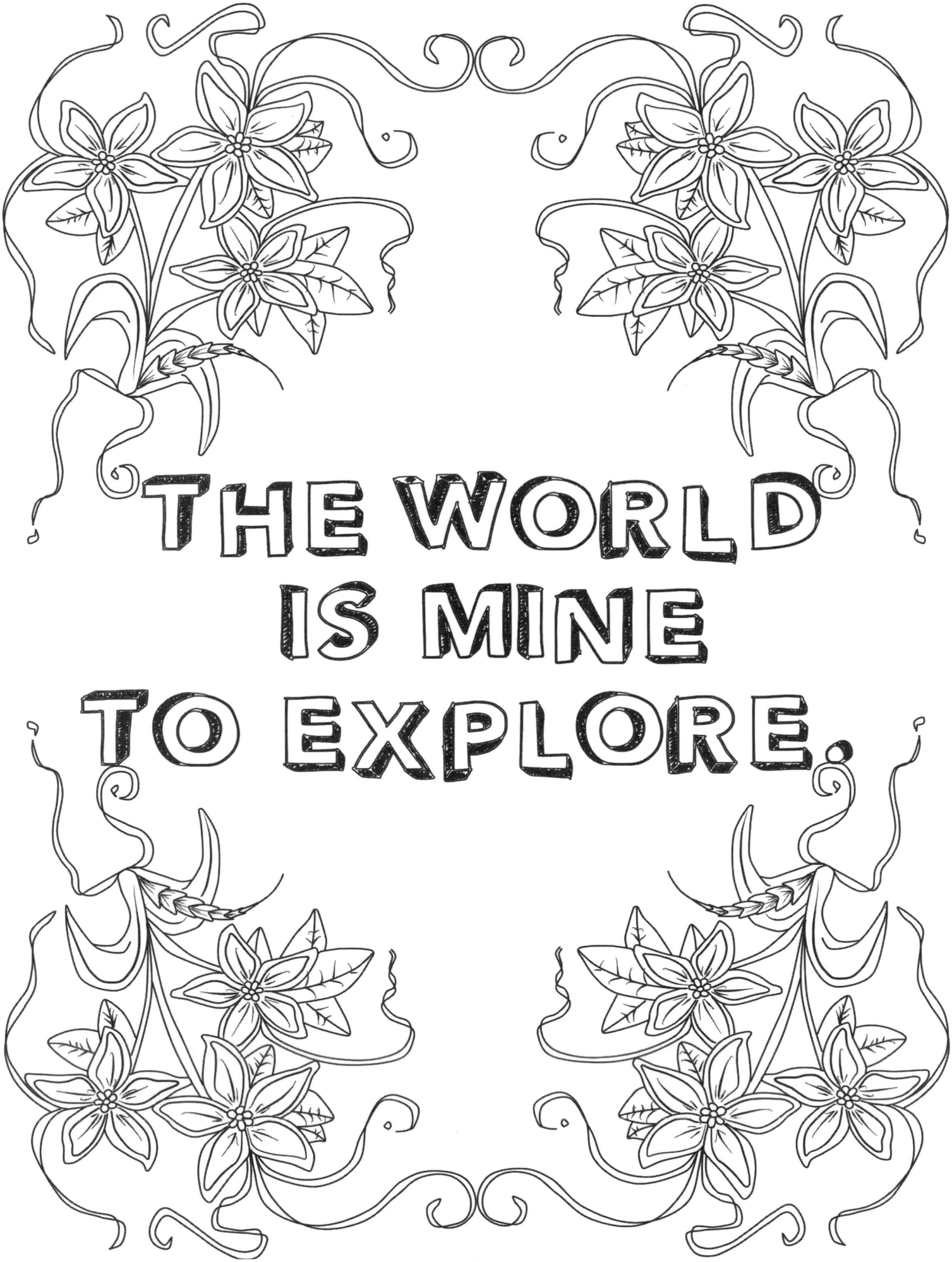
THE WORLD
IS MINE
TO EXPLORE.

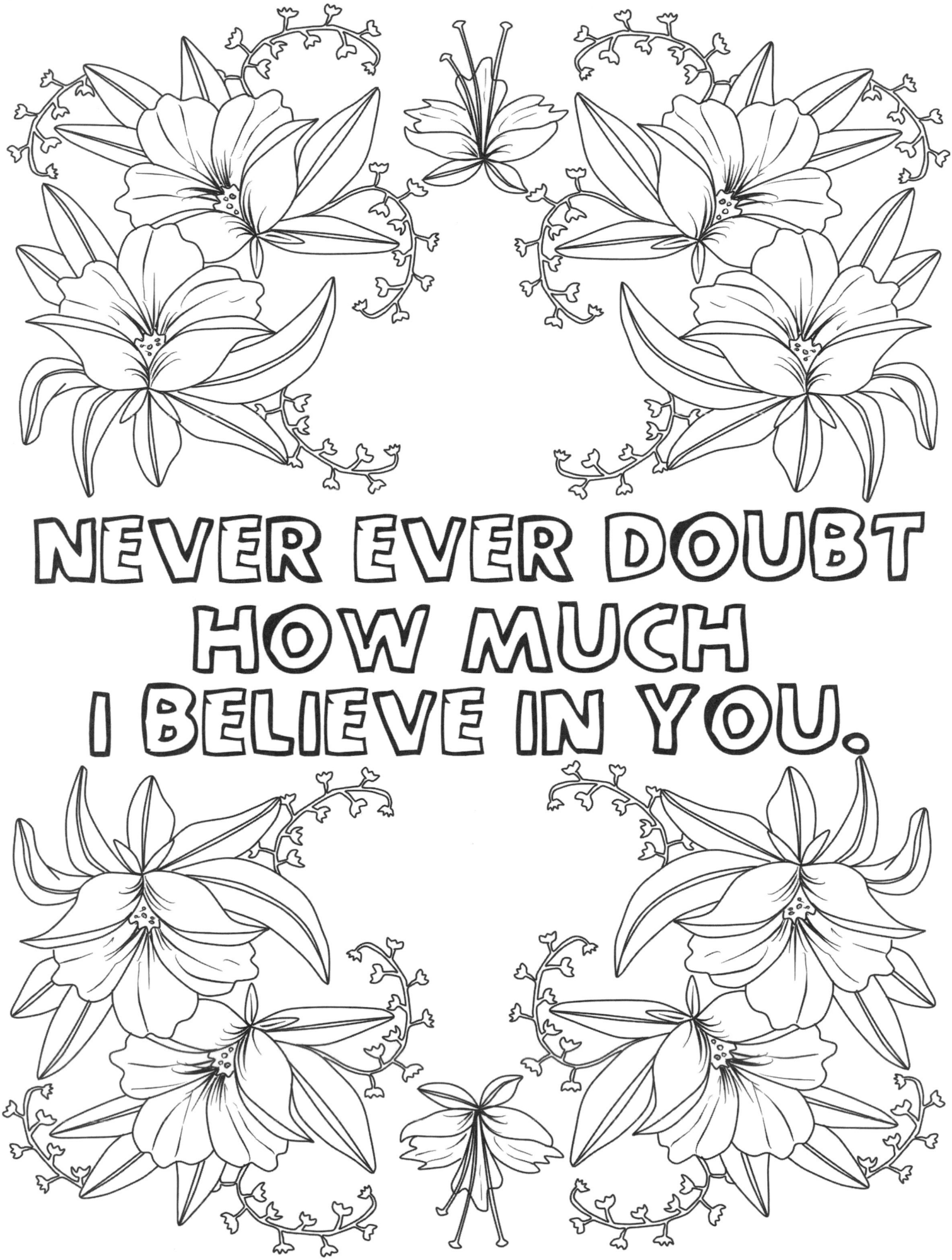
NEVER EVER DOUBT
HOW MUCH
I BELIEVE IN YOU.

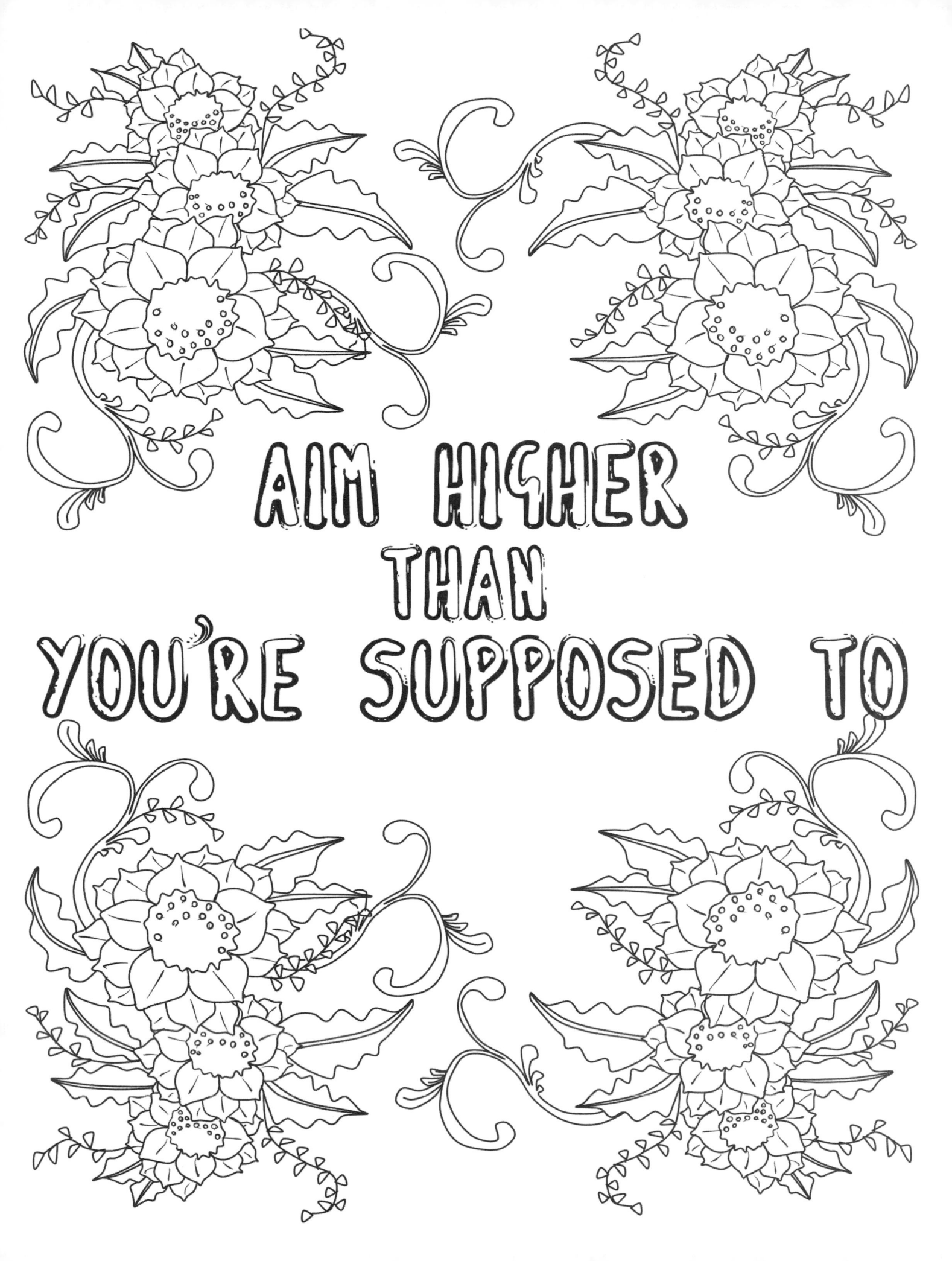
AIM HIGHER
THAN
YOU'RE SUPPOSED TO

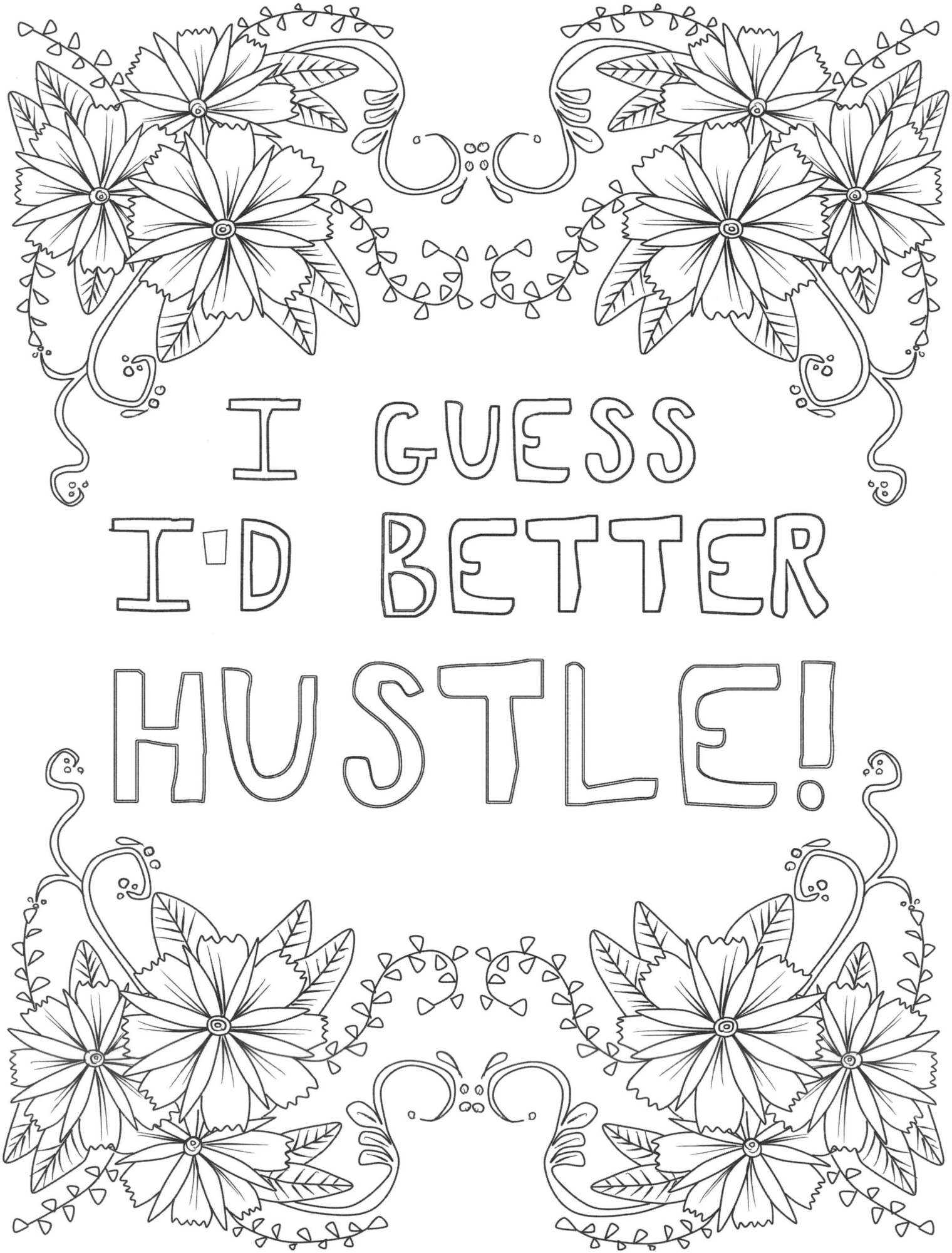
I GUESS
I'D BETTER
HUSTLE!